Godly
ANXIETY

Godly ANXIETY

Spiritual Tools
for Managing Anxiety

A WORKBOOK

LECIA CRIDER

Contents

Introduction

Have you met the Grip?

I bet you have. Maybe he visits you occasionally, or maybe he's practically your roommate. He might even be the reason you picked up this book.

You know him. He's that nameless dread that clutches at you from time to time. You feel him in your gut or around your heart. You might feel him in the pace of your breathing or your pulse. He might feel like sweat, or tears. He arrives unexpectedly and without invitation. Sometimes you know why he's there, sometimes not.

He is a physical manifestation of your anxiety.

This book is about godly anxiety. What is that? Well, to understand it let's look at a term you might be more familiar with: godly sorrow. You know that there are different reasons you might feel sorrow over sin. For example, you might feel sorry you got caught doing something wrong. You might feel sorry that you have to give up your favorite sins to be counted righteous, wishing God would allow just this one particular indiscretion (see Mormon 2:13). But *godly* sorrow is different. As Elder Neal A. Maxwell put it, "...a weekend of regret may produce some 'sorrowing of the damned,' but not the 'mighty change' which only godly sorrow produces".[1] Godly sorrow is sorrow that moves you to sanctifying action; action such as making restitution, confessing sin, and repenting sincerely. This kind of sorrow enriches our lives and brings us closer to our heavenly home.

Godly anxiety is much the same. When we allow our anxiety to *move us toward sanctifying action*, it can actually become a blessing. (Stay with me here!) When anxiety moves us to seek our God in more meaningful ways, to rivet our focus on the refuge of our Savior, to cling more tightly to the safety of our covenants, we are changed for the better, and the Grip loses his power over us.

If you battle anxiety, you probably already know you're not alone. People are talking about and sharing personal stories of their struggles with anxiety on social media with honesty and forthrightness. We hear about it at church and in conference talks. Life coaches and mission presidents alike address the issue regularly. It's certainly no coincidence that we hear more and more about anxiety these days. After all, the world we live in can be downright scary. There are wars, civil unrest, racial discord, refugee crises, faith crises, financial upheaval, natural disasters and even pandemics to worry about, just to name a few. The word "anxiety" can also help us explain how we're feeling when we're dealing with stress, worry, fear, regret, shame, insecurity, or dread, among others. I won't try to distinguish between all these closely related emotions in the context of this workbook. In fact, you'll find that I interchange some of those words pretty freely here, mainly because they feel so similar when we are experiencing them, and more importantly, because the tools we will discuss for managing anxiety apply to all its derivatives.

LDS Services (the social services arm of The Church of Jesus Christ of Latter-Day Saints) defines anxiety by saying, "Anxiety is a normal human emotion...It is part of the 'opposition in all things,' without which there would be no 'happiness nor misery...' It is part of our emotional alarm system. It motivates us to prepare for important events. It causes us to protect ourselves when we feel threatened. It enhances performance. It helps us make thoughtful decisions, solve problems, and prepare for challenges..." Relate this to a time when you had to give an important presentation at work or school. Being a bit anxious about the assignment would likely lead you to prepare and practice, things that will almost surely lead to a good presentation.

The definition continues, "*On the other hand*, there are also anxiety disorders. These interfere with our alarm system and its many benefits and are characterized by persistent, overwhelming, uncontrollable anxiety that impedes normal functioning."[2] Sticking with our presentation scenario, over-anxiety might lead to procrastination and paralysis, greatly impairing your chances of success.

Just as there are varied definitions of anxiety, so, too, do people experience it differently. Underline the descriptions you relate to most: it can feel like a crippling sense of inadequacy and the resulting insecurity that goes with that. It can be an inflated concern about what others think of us and our decisions and opinions. It might feel more like a nameless dread that strikes without warning. It manifests itself in our body as well as our mind, with symptoms that can include trembling, a racing heart, sweating, shortness of breath, a sour tightness in the stomach or chest, and lightheadedness, among others. It is generally based in the past, such as when we feel ambushed by memories that make us uncomfortable, or the future, like when we say, "But what if this horrible thing happens?"

There are those who wrestle with Big Moments of anxiety—times of such *sudden and complete overwhelm* that the ability to function is greatly impaired. I've only rarely experienced it that way, but often enough that I have no end of sympathy for those who grapple with Big Moments on a regular basis. For others, anxiety ebbs and flows around them as if they were pebbles in its stream: me, small; it, big.

Some experience anxiety in combination with illnesses like depression, bipolar disorder, OCD, or a variety of other mental health issues. Anxiety disorders often warrant professional help.

When I hit about forty years old, I realized anxiety was becoming my master, and I needed to do something about it. I read that "Anxiety gets progressively more intense as it goes along if you don't intervene,"[3] and I found that to be true in my life. It was time to intervene. Since I'm a very practical person, I wanted a workbook to get me started, some sort of step-by-step self-help program for gaining the upper hand on my anxiety. I knew if I just read a book, I would quickly forget it. Instead, I wanted something a little more hands on that would help me make actual changes in my life. I never found my workbook, but my search led me to discover some tools on my own that were enormously helpful. I will briefly touch on a variety of resources in a later chapter, but the main scope of this book will be spiritual. It's meant to be that very workbook I could never find, to help you take the sanctifying action that is most helpful for you, *as guided by the Spirit*.

You'll find here (along with plenty of stories) specific coping techniques, or spiritual tools, that I learned how to use through a prolonged study of anxiety and its antidotes in the scriptures and the words of the prophets. You'll find practical ways to follow Elder Jeffrey R. Holland's counsel to "[f]aithfully pursue the time-tested devotional practices that bring the Spirit of the Lord into your life" in times of mental or emotional challenge.[4] I recognize that for most of us spiritual tools will only be part of the solution, but they are the sure foundation, the place to begin building from, the very best place to *start*.

If you struggle with anxiety, you may sometimes wonder, "Can the Lord use me? Am I steady enough to serve Him? Do I need too much help myself to be a helper?" Take heart. Many powerful servants of God have been anxious or afraid. Consider this quote from the Relief Society General Board in 2019: "Of the 10 women on the Relief Society General Board, all have been affected by anxiety and depression."[5] We are not alone in our struggles, and with the Lord, we are all we need to be for any job.

When I heard Elder Gerrit Gong say in General Conference, "...counting sheep doesn't make me sleepy. I worry about missing or losing one, and that keeps me awake,"[6] I laughed quietly in recognition. *He has anxiety!* I thought. And yet, he is what I would call high achieving. In addition to what he faced in a high pressure political career, I'm sure he now faces incredible challenges in fulfilling his calling as a member of The Quorum of the Twelve Apostles. I would guess the need to stay extremely close to the Spirit is way up there. I'm confident he is the recipient of plenty of mocking and finger-pointing from those who occupy the great and spacious building. And yet, he does it. He does all he is supposed to do, even though he is anxious, at least some of the time.

It would seem possible that Elder Gong faces significantly more daily pressure than I do, and that he has at least some anxiety in his life, and yet he continues to be a powerful servant for the Lord, which is what I want for myself as well. So, it's possible. It's possible for you, and it's possible for me. In fact, I would guess that you're probably a much more useful servant to the Lord than you give yourself credit for. I really don't think you would have picked up this book if you weren't giving all you can give to being your best you.

So, lift up your head. Be of good cheer. You are right—there is no cure for anxiety. But I promise that you *can* serve God, fulfill your purposes in life, and yes, ***even find joy***, all while living with anxiety. Let's take a look at how it's done.

Chapter One

ALWAYS REMEMBER HIM

It was around 3 a.m., definitely too early to be awake, and yet there I was. Some small sound or maybe my husband stirring beside me had woken me up and, as usual, I wasn't going to be getting back to sleep anytime soon. Maybe you've noticed how the Grip hits with an especially heavy hand at night. Worries that seem small and manageable in the light of day become simply terrifying in the dark of night. I'm guessing that night I was thinking about a leaky faucet or some other soul-shattering emergency.

My solution for nights like this is to have a *go-to thought*. Go-to thoughts are just feel-good thoughts that you can have ready to go at any moment to combat The Grip. Thoughts about an event you're looking forward to, a visit with friends you're excited about, or maybe a really good vacation memory work pretty well. Sometimes it's easy for me to come up with a thought because we're about to go to the beach, or we just celebrated a holiday. But most of the time, my life is pretty mundane, and go-to thoughts are harder to come by. Also, I can only use a go-to thought so many times before it loses its effectiveness, kind of like a car loses that new car smell.

One night I stumbled on a fresh, new go-to thought. My kids had been learning the song "The Miracle" by Shawna Belt Edwards in Primary, and I began singing it in my mind. The song tells of the miracles Christ performed during his mortal life, and as I silently sang the lyrics, I pictured the events they describe. The miracles Christ performed, like walking on the water, calming the storm, and healing the blind man. Thinking through this song turned out to be really effective in calming my night anxiety, and I realized there is something particularly powerful in focusing my go-to thoughts on Christ. This was a new idea for me. I had never tried to focus my go-to thoughts like that before, although I promised to do so every week when I took the sacrament! Finally I started living the sacramental covenant I made weekly to "always remember Him," and I felt myself *unlocking powerful blessings*. Remember, the promise we are given when we keep our sacramental covenant is to "always have his Spirit" to be with us (D&C 20:77). This is one of the principles with a promise we see so often in the scriptures. We promise to always remember Him, and He promises to fill us with His spirit. And the fruits of having the Spirit with us include "love, joy, peace," among others (Galatians 5:22). As Elder Ulisses S. Soares taught, "happiness and peace in this life and in the world to come depend upon remembering the Savior and your covenants with Him daily."[7] Or, in this case, nightly. And frankly, it's much easier to come up with go-to thoughts about Christ than my own boring life!

I had stumbled on a spiritual tool, and as I began to study it more thoroughly, I was soon awestruck by the power of it.

There are many scriptural examples of the power of always remembering Him. One of my favorites is in 1 Nephi 11. Here, Nephi is pondering on his father's words about the Savior and the love of God when he receives an incredible visitation from the Spirit of the Lord, who asks him, basically, "What do you want?" Nephi desires knowledge from the Spirit. Specifically, he wonders what is the interpretation of the tree his father had seen in a dream? (vv.10-11).

Nephi doesn't actually receive a direct answer to his question. Instead of telling him the interpretation of the tree, the Spirit leads

Nephi through a grand vision of the life of Christ. Here comes the really interesting part. The Spirit still hasn't told Nephi anything about the interpretation of the tree, but after envisioning the Savior's birth (the ultimate expression of the Father's love), the Spirit again asks Nephi if he knows the meaning of the tree. Nephi answers simply, "Yea, it is the love of God..." (vv. 21-22). Nephi received the power of knowledge as he pondered the loving gift given by our Father of our Savior, Jesus Christ.

There are other examples of remembering the Savior as well.

Alma was rescued from the pit of despair in a most remarkable way by fixing his mind on and calling upon Jesus Christ.

After receiving a startling visit from an angel who called him to repentance, Alma could move neither limb nor mouth for three days and three nights. He wasn't just paralyzed, he was "racked with eternal torment," his soul was "harrowed up to the greatest degree" and he was "tormented with the pains of hell" (Alma 36:10-13). That sounds like a fairly anxious few days for Alma.

And yet, as soon as he remembered the prophecies of his father "concerning the coming of one Jesus Christ, a Son of God," his pains went away and he was filled with joy (vv. 18-20). Alma remembered Christ and he was blessed with joy and peace (the fruit of the Spirit).

In more recent times, author and speaker Merrilee Boyack was suffering from months of sleep deprivation due to severe anxiety. She finally made her way to a doctor who was a member of The Church of Jesus Christ of Latter-Day Saints, and, she writes, he "immediately gave me a proper diagnosis. But what he said next was a surprise. 'Merrilee, the most important thing you need to do is turn your anxiety over to God.'" The doctor invited her to spend time each day meditating on "The Living Christ: The Testimony of the Apostles." Sister Boyack describes what happened when she gave his suggestion sincere effort: "A thrill ran through me as I began to ponder the testimony of our great Healer and knew that I had found comfort and peace in my soul."[8] I tried this, too, memorizing small sections of "The Living Christ" to use at night, and they worked wonderfully well as go-to thoughts.

That's the power of always remembering Him, it's the power of the Atonement of Jesus Christ, and it's the first tool I'd like to give you for your toolbox.

My husband's precious Grandma was known to all of us as Gigi, short for Great-Grandma. When she passed, she left a big hole in our lives. I want my kids to remember her, but my youngest daughter, Alyza, was not quite three years old when Gigi passed away. How much do you remember from when you were two?!

Gigi and Alyza had a little routine that would play out each time we visited. By the time Alyza was old enough to walk and talk, Gigi was mostly confined to her bed, so we would visit with her in her bedroom. Each time Alyza appeared in her bedroom door, Gigi would cry out, "Oh, there's my little sweetie!" Alyza would then climb up in bed with her, get under covers, and snuggle up.

It's a precious memory for me, and I'd like it to be a precious memory for Alyza, too, but that's going to take some effort because she was so young. So how do I make sure Alyza will always remember Gigi?

Mostly, I talk about her. I tell that "Gigi story" often, and I remind Alyza and all of my children of Gigi's love for them and her continued involvement in their lives. We look at pictures of Gigi together and talk about how great it will be to see her again. I sometimes ask Heavenly Father if Gigi could be assigned to help my children—to be with my son on his mission, or to walk with my daughter to school. Indeed, one of my daughters had the sacred and unique experience of receiving help from Gigi when she was on our stake's pioneer trek. To be honest, I wasn't really all that surprised when she told me about it. Gigi loves her family!

Gigi wasn't just special to my kids; she was special to me. As a working mom with five children, her story mirrored mine, and I often asked her for advice on how to handle all the roles I was trying to fill. Now that I can't speak to her face to face anymore, I find myself asking, "What would Gigi do in this situation?"

These strategies to remember a grandmother are all ways we can remember Christ as well. We can look at pictures of Christ with our family. You don't have to spend a lot of money to have pictures of Christ in your home. There are beautiful ones printed in church magazines and in our Come Follow Me study manuals.

We can talk of Christ, telling our children stories of His life (2 Nephi 25:26). We can remind ourselves and our families of His love for us and His continued involvement in our lives.

I can say to my oldest daughter, "Remember when you fractured your elbow but didn't want to miss your choir concert that evening, so we went straight from urgent care to the performance hall? And remember how, as you sang Amazing Grace, you felt the grace of Christ lift your pain from you? And how your elbow didn't hurt anymore that night until you got in the car after the concert was over?" (And then it hurt A LOT!)

You have stories like that to tell. If you can't remember them, ask God to remind you. Thoughts will come into your mind, reminding you of ways *Christ has been involved in your life*. Write them down. Revisit them and add to them.

We can continually ask our Savior to help us. To be with us as we try to balance our bank statement, or when we give a presentation at work. To help us when we have three kids all throwing up at once, or when we don't think we can bear to play Candyland one more time. To give us the courage to fill out a college application after 15 years away from school, or to bear testimony when it's time to stand up for truth. We can ask for the Savior to be dispatched to our aid at any time. Even in the middle of the night, when small fears turn big.

And, of course, we can ask ourselves always, "What would Jesus do in this situation?"

I love Sister Sharon Eubank. I sit up a little straighter and open my notebook a little faster when I see her walk to the pulpit. Her talks speak to me, and never more so than when I heard her ask, "What are the *practical steps*...to reconnecting to the power of Jesus Christ?"[9] See, "practical" and "power" are two things I'm a bit obsessed with. Now you're imagining me as a super-villain who wants to take over the world. But, although I would like to take over the Cheetos factory for a day, that's not the kind of power that really captures my attention. I'm talking about the kind of power you get through the grace of Christ that allows you to be a force for good. I'm so, so not there yet, but I think about it a lot.

And practical? That should be my middle name. Far from getting angry at my husband when he gives me a practical gift, I actually ask for things like a new garden hose or a knife sharpener for my birthday. One of the best gifts my husband ever gave me was what I call my chainsaw on a stick. It's basically a chainsaw with an extra-long handle for reaching tree limbs, but it's powder blue and so much more useful than a bottle of French perfume. I love my chainsaw on a stick (and my husband)!

Needless to say, I was definitely interested in what Sister Eubank had to say about practical ways to tap into the power of Christ. She quoted President Nelson when he said, "*The key* is to make and keep sacred covenants...it is not a complicated way." Then Sister Eubank continued, "Make Christ the center of your life."[10]

Sounds relatively simple, and indeed, as President Nelson expressed, it's not complicated. But neither is it easy. Have you ever truly tried to always remember Him? I have. I lasted about 30 seconds before I got distracted by the dryer buzzing.

But then I read similar, covenant-centered advice from Sister Wendy Nelson that gave me a better idea how to keep Christ top of mind. She advised memorizing the words of our covenants and repeating them silently to ourselves when we need to connect with the powers of heaven. She related, "A dear friend recently did just that on a day when she didn't feel well and yet was less than one hour away from a major and highly stressful assignment. She wrote, 'As I waited alone in my car before the event, and because I physically didn't feel well, I chose to focus on the words of the initiatory. As those words went through my mind, I actually started to feel a little bit better. Plus, they gave me a feeling of peace and assurance that somehow I'd get through the assignment.' Just think of the power that is available to us in our sacred words of worship!"[11] If you are not able to attend the temple as often as you might need to memorize those covenantal words, focus instead on the meaning of a particular ordinance, or the words of the sacrament prayers. It's the act of *bringing your mind to a sacred place* that really invites the power of God into your situation.

Elder Kim B. Clark had similar advice: "We rivet our focus on Jesus Christ and His gospel by living our covenants."[12] I love that word 'rivet'. A rivet is a mechanical tool used to join two pieces of material together. What makes a rivet different from a screw or bolt is that it is a permanent fastener. When two items are riveted together, they stay together. When we rivet our focus on Christ, we stay with Him, we become a part of Him. And as we live our covenants (which simply means keeping the promises we have made to God) our everyday actions become a remembrance of Him.

Elder Gerrit W. Gong suggests another great way to remember Jesus Christ: "Gratefully remembering the assistance of others and the Spirit's guiding influence is a way we remember Him. It is a way we count our many blessings and see what God hath done."[13] When we acknowledge that our lives are constantly blessed in various ways, we are acknowledging our Savior, as He is the One doing the blessing.

It gives me comfort to think that maybe I don't need the mind discipline of a Jedi warrior to always remember Him. I'm remembering Him when I live my covenants by sitting and mourning with a friend who's experienced a loss; when I help a neighbor child who's fallen off a bike; when I give of my time, talents or resources to attend the temple or fulfill a calling, or when I'm grateful for those who have helped me in similar ways.

Remembering Christ through keeping our covenants, as Sister Nelson and Elder Clark advised, brings power into our lives. Read these verses from Mosiah 24 with the bondage of anxiety in mind:

"And it came to pass that the voice of the Lord came to them in their afflictions, saying: Lift up your heads and be of good comfort, for I know of the covenant which ye have made unto me; and I will covenant with my people and deliver them out of [their] bondage [of anxiety].

And I will also ease the burdens which are put upon your shoulders, that even you cannot feel them upon your backs, even while you are in bondage [to anxiety]; and this will I do that ye may stand as witnesses for me hereafter, and that ye may know of a surety that I, the Lord God, do visit my people in their afflictions" (vv. 13-14, my additions in brackets).

Elder David A. Bednar says about these verses: "Note the centrality of covenants to the promise of deliverance...for in the ordinances of the priesthood, the power of godliness is manifest unto men and women in the flesh, including the blessing of the Atonement."[14]

As Enos said after asking the Lord for some special promises, "I...knew it would be according to the covenant which he had made; wherefore my soul did rest" (Enos 1:17).

But Elder Bednar continues, "I wonder if we fail to fully acknowledge this strengthening aspect of the Atonement in our lives and mistakenly believe we must carry our load all alone—through sheer grit, willpower, and discipline with our obviously limited capacities."

We forget, or maybe we don't really know, like Enos did, what kind of power our covenants carry. So, we do the carrying instead. And you can sometimes go a long time like that and still function, carrying the load all on your own. Grit, willpower and discipline are admirable traits. It's just that they're so very, very tiring. Honestly—*aren't you tired* from trying to go it alone?

It's this physical sensation of being exhausted at times from mistakenly carrying my own spiritual burdens that connects me so intimately to the woman with the issue of blood in the New Testament. You may be familiar with her story. According to Luke, she had been sick for twelve—twelve!—years, and had spent all her money going from doctor to doctor, but nobody could heal her (Luke 8:43). Mark adds to the picture by intimating that many doctors had taken her money and, instead of making her better, had actually made her worse (Mark 5:26). So imagine her exhaustion. Twelve years of losing blood had almost certainly made her anemic, a symptom of which is extreme fatigue. She had grave financial concerns. Even worse, she was considered unclean because of her bleeding, and thus wasn't supposed to be mingling in a crowd anyway, so she probably had plenty of shame and anxiety over that to go with the rest. It's no wonder that reaching out and touching the hem of Christ's garment was the most she could do.

Yes, there could have been many reasons for her slight touch. The crowd, her status as an unclean person—but don't you think she might have just been really, profoundly tired? *Don't you think it took everything she had that day to lift her hand to that sacred hem?* That might be how you're feeling today, too. As if just lifting your hand might do you in. And how can you ask for help when the asking itself could crack you into pieces? But when she did it, when she reached out to Christ, she "felt in her body that she was healed" and Christ felt strength go out of Him, to her. It was a literal, physical transference of His power.

He took her burden, and she was immediately strengthened by Him. I believe this can happen as literally for us as it did for her when we reach out to Christ, and *always remember Him.* I invite you to reach out right now, before you read any further. Maybe in this moment you feel too tired to pray. I've been there, when the thought of moving to your knees is just too much. So, don't. Don't move. Reach out from right where you are, right now. Try just saying simply, "Lord, give me strength." Say it often, throughout the day and night, and watch what happens.

Let me introduce you to "me-work". Me-work is the part where you get to take those sanctifying actions that turn everyday anxiety into godly anxiety; where you put the tools in your toolbox to work. It's like homework, but it's all about improving your own life, so I call it me-work. Plus, the word homework is an anxiety trigger for many people and I would never do that to you! Please spend time on the me-work—it's what makes this book different from all the other books you've already read and forgotten about.

Me-Work: Explore the power of pondering

Pondering is giving your mind quiet time to reflect. It's similar to meditation in that you want to minimize outside distractions and meandering thoughts. But instead of focusing on your breath or repeating a mantra, you focus on working through a particular thought, topic, or question you have.

Pondering is a great way to spend time with Christ at the center of your thoughts, remembering Him. It creates quiet space for God to speak to us. As the Psalm says, "Be still, and know that I am God" (46:10). Or these verses from 1 Kings: "And, behold, the Lord passed by, and a great and strong wind rent the mountains, and brake in pieces the rocks before the Lord; but the Lord was not in the wind: and after the wind an earthquake; but the Lord was not in the earthquake: And after the earthquake a fire; but the Lord was not in the fire: and after the fire a still, small voice" (1 Kings 19:11-12).

If God speaks to us with a still, small voice, how can we expect to hear Him with music blaring, kids playing, the TV on, our phones in front of our faces, and maybe all of those at once? The answer is... we usually can't. We need to carve out quiet time for Him.

Pondering should be intentional and not just a quick decision not to turn the radio on when you're driving, although that's good, too! Author Joni Hilton says, "Pondering is not simply sitting still and letting your mind wander. It's a focused concentration on things of eternity, on matters of the spirit. It's weighing and deliberating, reaching with our minds to a higher level, for higher answers. It can open our eyes to spiritual understanding and unlock revelation."[15]

In other words, ponder to hear God's voice, not just to think. The best part is, you can do it from anywhere, even in your favorite chair, snuggled up under a blanket. Don't get me wrong—pondering is hard. Not only does it take concentration of thought, but it feels a lot like doing nothing, which equates to "wasting time" for many of us. But *pondering can bring real power to everything else we do.* So, if you have a hard time being still, try to keep that in mind—the power you are adding to your other activities by connecting with God is *productive* time.

Tips for pondering:

1. Be alone
2. Minimize distractions
3. Decide what topic to focus on and a minimum time frame for your pondering
4. Ask questions
5. Write your impressions

You can most certainly ponder on a particular challenge you are having, like anxiety, but it can also be very powerful to ponder your blessings, who you could serve and how, or especially the life and sacrifice of Jesus Christ.

Jot your thoughts down as you take a minute to ponder right now. Here's a question you could ask to get you started: "How can I connect with Christ today?"

_____

_____

_____

_____

_____

_____

_____

_____

_____

_____

_____

_____

Scripture Power

Let's study D&C 6:36

"Look unto me in every thought; doubt not, fear not."

Which words strike you most in this scripture? Underline them. Why do those words speak to you? What do they mean to you?

_____

_____

_____

_____

_____

_____

_____

_____

_____

_____

_____

_____

Chapter Two

PEACE

At the age of ten, my son Trevin went through a phase where he wanted to bear his testimony in church every month, and he always had something, ummm, interesting to say. He's in his twenties now, and I still have the occasional ward member who wants to reminisce with me about those testimonies of his. It was a precious time.

I remember one Fast Sunday in particular. The week prior we'd had a visiting authority, Elder Richard Hinckley, in town for stake conference. Trevin and I had been learning about spiritual gifts together, and he wondered if Elder Hinckley might have the gift of healing, which could really help my husband, who suffers from chronic pain. Trevin began to earnestly pray that Elder Hinckley would give his dad a healing blessing while he was in town.

I was beside myself with anxiety over this faithful prayer of my son. There were many people in our stake with bigger problems, so why would Elder Hinckley come visit us? I worried over this incessantly. Lacking the faith of my son, I wondered if I should intervene. Sitting with a friend after the Saturday night adult session of conference, I confided in her about Trevin's hopeful prayer. Not being one to sit around, my friend immediately took my son's story up to the stake presidency on the stand. The good news was relayed back to me—Elder Hinckley would come!

Knowing he was leaving town after our Sunday meetings the next morning, I was sure he would be coming by that night, so I did what any woman would do. I raced home to clean the house! I told the kids the exciting news, and they all pitched in. Trevin was beyond thrilled that his prayer was being answered, and I only felt a smidge guilty for my inability to leave it in the Lord's hands. We waited up until 10:00 p.m., when I reluctantly sent the kids to bed, promising Trevin I would wake him when Elder Hinckley arrived. Then I sat and worried, which I'm very good at, by the way. By 11:00 p.m. I was in tears and by midnight my last shred of hope was gone. Nobody was coming, and I did not know how I was going to explain this to my young son. I didn't sleep much that night, and the next morning I got up early and cried some more, then got down on my knees to plead with my Father in Heaven. I know Him as a generous God who gives me so, so much, but this time I was asking Him for the one thing I rarely get—an explanation. An explanation I could pass on to my son so his faith would not be shattered.

Now, I'm not joking here—my phone rang the minute I said amen. It was President Jackson of the stake presidency. As the conversation started (with me trying to hide that fact that I had been crying), I quickly realized there had been a miscommunication. The stake presidency had understood that my husband Jay needed a blessing, and President Jackson was calling to make an appointment to come by and do that. The part about Elder Hinckley had not hit its mark, they just didn't know that part of the request. Therefore, Elder Hinckley also never knew of Trevin's request, and he wasn't coming.

I was so grateful for the explanation. I mean, I was so beyond *thrilled* to get an explanation! I told President Jackson we would love to have him come and bless Jay. When Trevin woke up, I was able to tell him that Heavenly Father was in fact sending someone to bless his dad, and perhaps it would be the very best person for the job.

Indeed, President Jackson gave my husband a beautiful and inspired blessing.

The next Sunday, my young son got up to bear his testimony as usual. I'll never forget it. He leaned forward onto the podium and gave the congregation the solemn look of a much older person. Then he said, very soberly, "I'm here to testify that Jesus works in *verrry mysterious ways.*"

Yes, He does, doesn't He? Perhaps that's because He sees what we don't see, and understands what we don't understand. "My thoughts are not your thoughts, neither are your ways my ways, saith the Lord" (Isaiah 55:8). And aren't we glad? Where would we be if our own thoughts, ideas and solutions were the very best the universe could come up with? These days I try to interfere a little bit less in the faith process, and let my awesome, omniscient, all-powerful Father in Heaven do His thing without getting in the way. It's still a regular temptation for me to try to control things, but I try to recognize this as a misguided attempt to control my anxiety, which is a bit like me trying to take command of the Nephite army when Captain Moroni is standing right there. Foolish! *Let God be God. He's very good at it.*

The almighty vision, power and grace of our Lord Jesus Christ is one reason He bears the title The Prince of Peace (Isaiah 9:6). We can be at peace when we realize we can trust Him to always do what's best for us, precisely because, like His Father, He can see the end from the beginning. *We don't always get an explanation for the hard things in our lives, but that doesn't mean there isn't one.* "But behold, all things have been done in the wisdom of him who knoweth all things" (2 Nephi 2:24). We don't need to control what He does for us; we just need to partake of His peace.

Luckily, the scriptures give a ton of guidance about how to do this. Let's study it out together for a minute.

D&C 19:23 is a good place to start. The Savior invites, "Learn of me, and listen to my words; walk in the meekness of my Spirit." When we accept and act upon that invitation, we receive His promise:

"you shall have peace in me." This is another clear example of a principle with a promise. You do these three things, and I will give you peace. As we know, the Lord is bound when we do what He says (D&C 82:10). Meaning, He is bound by his very nature to keep His promises to us. Were He to break a promise, that would make Him a liar. And God cannot lie (see Hebrews 6:18). Therefore, if He says that He will give us peace if we learn of Him, listen to His words, and walk in the meekness of His spirit, He will. I invite you to try the Lord's word and see what happens.

So how do we really incorporate those three directions into our lives, so we can obtain the hoped-for promise? Let's break it down.

Learn of me

Peace comes from learning about our Savior, His character, His love for us, and His covenantal mission to redeem each of us, to bring us home. As we learn of Him, our trust in Him grows, and that *trust is the very foundation of peace.*

I love how the Doctrine and Covenants is so full of the first-person voice of Christ. It makes this particular book of scripture seem so intimate. You'll also find His voice throughout the other books of scripture, and that's part of what makes the scriptures such a great place to start if you are trying to learn of Him; you can immerse yourself in His language.

My youngest daughter, Alyza, was in a Spanish immersion program in her elementary school from 1st through 4th grade. Each year, she had two teachers. She spent the morning with her English-speaking teacher, studying Language Arts and Social Studies. She spent the afternoon with her Spanish-speaking teacher, where she studied math and science.

Alyza, who is a good student with a smart brain, never learned much Spanish, despite 4 years of classroom instruction.

On the other hand, my son Daylon spent two years in Chile as a missionary. He spent only a few weeks in a classroom learning the language, but Daylon speaks Spanish fluently.

The difference in their ability could come from many things (including age), but I believe it mainly comes from the process of immersion. Daylon left his few weeks of classroom instruction and went to a country where he was fully immersed in the Spanish language for nearly two years. His companion spoke Spanish, as did the people they interacted with each day. He continued to study the language every morning, and he practiced using it *every* day.

Alyza, meanwhile, was anything but immersed. Although the program she was in is called "Spanish immersion," I was in her classroom enough to know that her Spanish-speaking teacher switched to English quite a bit, to help the kids understand what she was asking them to do. After school, Alyza came home to a family that speaks English exclusively. So exclusively that I had to use Google Translate to help her with her homework! She had little to no chance to practice using Spanish outside of the classroom.

So, to learn of Jesus Christ most effectively, I suggest immersion. Don't get scared. I don't mean you have to spend 24 hours a day reading your scriptures! But when you do read them, allow yourself to get immersed. Don't worry about how much you read. Read a couple of verses and let them wash over you. Stop and think, let the words flow around in your head for a bit. Use the pondering skills you've been practicing. Ask a question that comes to your mind, and listen for an answer as you become still, immersed. Read a few more verses. Write your questions and thoughts down.

Remember that scripture time can be highly personalized. You don't have to read from beginning to end. I hereby give you permission to spend a whole month on one chapter if you want. You can skip around. You can read a conference talk and then read the scripture references in the footnotes. You can read the Bible Dictionary—it's very enlightening! You don't even have to read, you can listen.

Immersion in the scriptures requires a bit of quiet time. I know that can be incredibly hard to come by, but here are a few suggestions: read a few verses and think about them while you rock your baby; make the scriptures the first thing you read in the morning—if you normally open your phone first, open to the scriptures before you look at anything else; switch out ten minutes of social media scrolling for 10 minutes of scripture immersion; listen in the car or while you're on a walk; if your kids are old enough to be readers, get the whole family involved in 10 minutes of (semi-quiet) reading before bed.

Other ways to immerse yourself in the word of God include having a Christ-centered playlist of music, listening to BYU devotionals or uplifting podcasts, and reading or listening to conference talks and gospel-themed books. You'll come up with your own great ideas as you begin the process of immersion.

A few months ago, the light switch in my bathroom broke. It was on and wouldn't turn off. I had no idea how to fix it, but being too cheap to call a repairman for something so small, I determined that I would learn how to replace the light switch. My go-to for situations like this is, of course, YouTube. I quickly found a video that walked me through the process, and I was able to successfully complete the repair, with only one extra trip to the hardware store.

I learned how to do this repair by copying someone who had been there, done that—my YouTube guide. Similarly, we learn of Christ as we attempt to "copy" what He has done. There are, of course, some things only He could do. But we can emulate many of his actions. We can reach out to those who are different from us. We can embrace the repentant. We can invite questions. We can bear testimony. We can listen. In this way, as we try to model ourselves after our Savior, we learn of Him.

It's worth noting that I could have watched that video about how to change my light switch a million times, I could have memorized every step, but unless I took action, my light switch was never going to work. Which brings us to the next phrase in our scripture: "listen to my words." Great peace comes from really listening to God's word and actively living a life that is in harmony with His commandments.

Listen to my words

When we complain that our kids aren't listening to us, usually we are actually complaining that they aren't *obeying* us. Often, they do hear us, they just choose to ignore what they're hearing!

Could our Heavenly Father ever say that about us? I know for sure there have been times when He could say that He'd like me to be more obedient.

In fact, there have been Sundays when I have approached the ordinance of the sacrament with an attitude of discouragement. I remember one Sunday in particular when I just felt horrible. I was so tired of repenting of the same sins all the time. I felt ashamed and incredibly weak and thought I must surely be a major disappointment to my Heavenly Parents.

However, God is good, and He allowed the Holy Ghost to tutor me a bit during the sacrament that week. As I sat in the semi-quiet environment of the chapel, my mind fixed on the Plan of Salvation. In particular, I thought about the "plan" part of it. Our Father in Heaven knew mortality would be hard; that it would, in fact, be impossible for us to travel the path without making some mistakes and getting some scars. So, He planned for that. He provided for us a Savior, Jesus Christ, and he set up certain cleansing ordinances that reflect the power of Christ's Atonement onto us, including baptism, the sacrament, and the initiatory ordinance in the temple.

The thought came to me very forcefully that by approaching the sacrament table humbly but under the burden of sin, *I was participating in the Plan of Salvation just like I was supposed to*. It is part of what was planned. Should my discouragement over my sins ever keep me away—away from church, away from the sacrament table, and away from my Savior's cleansing power—that is when I need to worry. That is when I am no longer living the Plan.

Certainly I have an obligation, as a disciple of Christ, to try to be continually improving and growing, but there will never be a Sunday—there will never be any day—when I don't need the Savior's Atonement. And that's okay because that's the Plan.

I am learning to more fully appreciate the gift that is repentance, even as I am working to be more obedient. Obedience is an expression of our love for Jesus Christ: "If ye love me, keep my commandments" (John 14:15). And so, truly listening to Christ's words means following Christ's counsel. As we immerse ourselves in the scriptures, we can read them actively. Meaning, we read with the intent to act on what we learn.

Listening *and* *o*beying bring other gifts into our lives in addition to peace. President Benson put it this way, "When obedience ceases to be an irritant and becomes our quest, in that moment God will endow us with power."[16] And Elder Hales said, "Obedience makes us progressively stronger, capable of faithfully enduring tests and trials in the future."[17] And from President Monson, "Obedience is a hallmark of prophets; it has provided strength and knowledge to them throughout the ages. It is essential for us to realize that we, as well, are entitled to this source of strength and knowledge. It is readily available to each of us today as we obey God's commandments."[18] And this wonderful statement from the scriptures, "...[King Benjamin] had taught them to keep the commandments of God, that they might rejoice and be filled with love towards God and all men" (Mosiah 2:4). Those are some mighty gifts from obedience: power, strength, faith, knowledge, joy and love.

As we learn of Christ and listen to His words, our faith in Him grows, and we begin to trust him enough to do the things He's asked us to do—even if we don't always understand why. This trust allows us to feel peace even during times of trouble.

Walk in the meekness of my Spirit

The scripture we are focusing on in this chapter, D&C 19:23, was the youth theme for 2018, and I love how the phrase "walk in the meekness of my Spirit" was introduced in church magazines. Because honestly—that one's a little hard to understand. Here's what I read: "Learning and listening describe what we need to do. Walking in the meekness of His Spirit is how we need to do it."[19] I love that!

The word that helps me understand meekness best is willingness. The Guide to the Scriptures defines meekness as being "Godfearing, righteous, humble, teachable, and patient under suffering. The meek are willing to follow gospel teachings." I think of it as a willingness to follow in Christ's footsteps.

Having a visual of this can be helpful. Imagine for a moment that you are walking on the road a few feet behind Jesus Christ. The beautiful, powerful light of His spirit radiates out from Him and flows back to you, bathing you in it. You are now walking *in* His spirit, and it feels incredibly wonderful. Pause and try to image that for a moment.

To stay within that glorious pool of light, you have to follow right behind Him. So, if He turns right, you turn right. If He veers left, you veer left. You follow in His footsteps, going where He goes and doing what He does. You notice that what He does is love others. He humbly does His Father's will. He accepts suffering with patience. He walks in perfect meekness. As you follow Him, basking in His light, you are now walking in the meekness of His spirit. What a holy place to be.

Never let admonitions to be obedient, meek, a disciple of Christ, or any of the other many invitations to improve that we receive as members of The Church of Jesus Christ of Latter-Day Saints add to your anxiety. When you are tempted to think of these invitations as to-dos that weigh you down, go back to the road you just imagined. For a moment, in your mind, walk that holy path again, cushioned and carried and borne up on wings by the essence of His spirit which surrounds you. Can you feel it?

Learn of me. Listen to my words. Walk in the meekness of my spirit. These invitations are a gift, and accepting them comes with a prize: peace.

Give it a try. Immerse yourself in the scriptures for a few minutes every day, be obedient, walk the path with Christ, and find peace.

Me-Work: Right-Size Goals

Just to make sure you don't feel overwhelmed with the invitation to learn of Him, listen to Him, and walk with Him, let's talk about setting right-sized goals: goals that are just right for you.

You've heard the usual description of a good goal. They say your goal should be SMART – Specific, Measurable, Attainable, Relevant and Time-Bound. That advice is completely perfect for a lot of people. Specifically, goal driven people. I hate that advice. I don't hate goal-driven people. I wish I was in their tribe. But I tend to go back and forth between living my status quo, and then throwing myself at a project with everything I have, often without really thinking it through first. Picture a freight train. It's either parked at the station, or it's barreling down the track. That's me.

I do have a goal setting standard that I hold myself to, although I admit it's somewhat less rigorous than the SMART standard. And my acronym is annoyingly inefficient—too many words. Nevertheless, here it is: I set BAND goals. That stands for Bite-size, Able to be changed, Not exhausting and Do-over-able. I think those are all pretty self-explanatory.

If this kind of goal setting sounds more your speed, I invite you to set some here today. I've helped you out with a little example of my own, although it may change...

Goal: Come to know Christ better

*B*ite size action: Listen to one conference talk a day—in the car, while I'm working, etc. I spend a lot of hours in front of a computer every day, so one 20-minute conference talk really is bite size in this case.

*A*ble to change: Reading is also okay

*N*ot exhausting: I'll give myself two freebies per week—days I can miss without guilt for any reason whatsoever

*D*o-over-able: If I miss more than my allotted number of guilt-free days, I will continue to be guilt-free and will just pick up where I left off the next day.

You see? My goal is important to me, but I'm not going to sacrifice my mental health on the altar of doing this one thing perfectly. I might be perfect at it. Or I might miss a few days here and there. But any number of days that I listen to a conference talk is better than zero, right? I can't find the downside to giving myself some grace in my goal setting.

Update: Like any decent writer who knows her first draft will almost certainly be trash, I let a few weeks go by between writing this manuscript and then picking it up again to edit it. I thought you might be interested to know how I've been doing on my goal in those few weeks.

A. I was surprised to learn I had set this goal; I had forgotten about it.

B. But before I forgot it was a goal, I did bookmark a site on my computer that has all the General Authority's talks and devotionals on it in chronological order and got into the habit of using it (bencrowder.net. Thanks, Ben).

C. I continue to be a freight train. I go many days without listening to a single conference talk, and then in a single day

I'll listen to four in a row (usually while I'm paying bills for work, which is a mind-numbing task).

D. I'm quite pleased with myself and actually do think I've grown closer to Christ, even though my method has been somewhat haphazard and I forgot that what I was doing started out as a goal!

So take heart and set a BAND goal today, maybe one that will help you learn of Christ more deeply, or hear His words more completely, or walk in His footsteps more often.

Scripture Power

Let's study John 14: 27
"Peace I leave with you, my peace I give unto you;
not as the world giveth, give I unto you. Let not your
heart be troubled, neither let it be afraid."

How would you define the peace the world offers?

_____

_____

_____

_____

_____

_____

_____

How is the peace of Christ different?

_____

_____

_____

_____

_____

_____

_____

How can embracing the peace of Christ change your life?

_____

_____

_____

_____

_____

_____

_____

Chapter Three

TRUST

If phobias and anxiety go hand-in-hand, then I'm just another typical story. I have a horrible fear of heights. Or, as my son likes to say, a horrible fear of gravity. I've tried numerous times to so-called "face my fear," and it doesn't work, at least not for me. I have braved the occasional roller coaster, climbed up on my plant shelf at least once a decade to dust it, and one year I even got on the roof to watch fireworks. Still scared.

A few years ago, I started out on what I thought would be an uneventful hike around the base of Mount St. Helens in Washington with my brother Rich and my sister Tricia. Before long we came to a very narrow passage, bordered on one side by the wall of the mountain, and on the other by a steep plunge into what I could only assume was oblivion. My siblings didn't even notice it and walked across at their usual clip, but I became paralyzed with fright and would not cross the narrow passage for several minutes. Rich and Tricia got a nice break while I wrestled with my demons! I believe they were really enjoying their break. At least, I know I heard laughter. Anyway, I finally made it across by plastering my body to the side of the mountain and inching my way sideways along the passage, with Tricia guarding the steep side so I wouldn't fall into oblivion.

This is the kind of story where a picture speaks a thousand words:

So, yes, I'm hamming it up a bit for the photos, but that is actually how Tricia and I traversed that passage! I admit, I was shocked when I first saw this photo, because it changed my perspective. I could suddenly see that I had never been in any real danger, and the cliff I was so afraid of was actually more of a slope. My siblings had assured me at the time that I was perfectly safe, but I thought I knew best, and what I knew was that I was risking my life! My faulty perspective caused me a lot of unnecessary anxiety and stress, and I slowed us all down and delayed our arrival at our intended destination.

That story reminds me of my mom's favorite scripture, Proverbs 3:5-6. "Trust in the Lord with all thine heart; and lean not unto thine own understanding. In all thy ways acknowledge him, and he shall direct thy paths."

On my hike with Rich and Tricia, I let fear direct my path. Not only did I lean heavily into the side of that mountain, I leaned into and accepted my own limited perspective, which was distorted by my fear. The path in front of me appeared to be dangerous and unpassable, when in fact it was not.

In dealing with our anxiety, which way do we lean? *Do we lean into our own distorted, fearful thoughts and believe them? Or do we lean into Christ, and believe Him?*

In her April 2017 General Conference talk, Bonnie Cordon said, "When we *physically* lean toward one side or another, we move off center, we are out of balance, and we tip. When we *spiritually* lean to our own understanding, we lean away from our Savior. If we lean, we are not centered; we are not balanced; we are not focused on Christ."[20]

I practice yoga in my living room most mornings. As I face the front of my mat, I am looking right at a beautiful painting of the Savior that hangs on the wall. When I attempt to do balance poses, this is the picture I focus on to keep from tipping over. In yoga talk, it's my drishti. The basic concept of drishti is that by fixing the gaze on an unmoving point, you can assume the characteristics of that point, becoming stable and balanced. Isn't that a beautiful way to think of Christ? As we focus on and lean into Him—our unmoving Friend— we take on His characteristics, becoming stable and balanced.

Sister Cordon also reminded us that in the premortal life we trusted the Savior. Imagine, for a minute, what it must have been like, hearing the Plan for the first time. I sometimes think it may have been a bit like being called on a mission to Mars, where our transportation would disintegrate upon arrival, but we were promised a rescue spacecraft would come and usher us safely back home. How much would you have to trust the people in charge of that rescue mission? To trust that they would do what they said they would do, that they would really come, and the plan would really work?

That's how much we had to trust our Savior, only more, since the stakes were obviously much higher—our eternal lives. We must have believed that He would do what He said He would do. That He would truly come, that He would, in fact, usher us safely back home. In our premortal existence, we must have trusted Him implicitly, or we wouldn't be here.

Now think of it. At this point, we *know* that He came. His life and ministry, death and resurrection have been recorded by many witnesses. He's already been here, and everything He needed to do to usher us safely home has been done. Should we trust Him any less now? Is there any reason why we should think that, after all He has already done, all the promises He has already kept, all the pain He has already endured for us, that He would choose *now* to abandon us?

Elder Richard G. Scott said, "To trust means to obey willingly without knowing the end from the beginning."[21] That is what we did in the spirit world. We didn't really *know* how things would all work out. We didn't have a perfect knowledge that Christ would perform His role as the Savior of all mankind without any deviations. But we trusted He would. And He did.

That trustworthy, infallible Christ is the same Savior who watches over us now. This is He who sees us in our trials and promises that everything will work out for our good in the end. Can we trust that He is right?

I have a favorite Old Testament story that really speaks to this point. It's the story of Jehoshaphat and his people, found in 2 Chronicles, Chapter 20. Every time I read this story, I'm just filled with a spirit of confidence and trust in the Lord.

Jehoshaphat was king of Judah some 850 years before the birth of Christ. At one point during his reign, he was warned that a great army was gathering to attack his people. How did the king react to this news? Well, verse 3 states simply, "And Jehoshaphat feared." Those few words are what make this scripture account so very real to me, because that's my first reaction to most unpleasant news as well.

But here's the lesson. In the very next breath, verse 3 also tells us that he "set himself to seek the Lord." When I picture King Jehoshaphat setting himself to seek the Lord, I picture him turning his face to the Lord with great resolve. He may have said to himself, "This situation is dire, and I will do whatever it takes to receive direction from the Lord on this matter."

And he does. He calls all his people to gather themselves together to fast and call upon the Lord and ask for His help. He goes to the temple to converse with the Lord. He calls upon all he knows about the character of the God he worships. He remembers the many times the Lord has saved his people in the past from invaders and from famine (vv. 3-9).

Then he tells the Lord about the grave situation he and his people are in. He confesses that they are too weak to have any hope of winning this battle on their own. He even concedes that they simply don't know what to do. Again, that seems very familiar and real to me. But he adds this important, humble declaration: *"our eyes are upon thee"* (vs. 12).

The Lord inspires one of the temple workers present, Jahaziel, with an answer. "Thus saith the Lord unto you, Be not afraid nor dismayed by reason of this great multitude: for the battle is not yours but God's" (vv. 14-15).

Be honest. How many of you are thinking right now, "Man, I wish someone would walk up to me and tell me exactly what the Lord wants me to hear." Perhaps He has. Perhaps that insight that Jahaziel gave to Jehoshaphat was recorded for the specific purpose that you might read those words today and feel peace about your own situation. As former Young Women General President Ardeth G. Kapp has said, the scriptures are like "letters from home."[22] Maybe you just received some mail.

Back to the story. The Lord continues his instructions to the king through Jahaziel. "You shall not need to fight this battle: set yourselves, stand ye still, and see the salvation of the Lord with you" (vs. 17).

And the Lord meant that literally. Jehoshaphat's people were to gather at a certain place in the wilderness, "out before the army" (vs. 21), and...be still. Can you imagine? Walk out in front of this giant army that wants to slay you and just stand there. Those were their instructions.

I'm humbled and amazed by how the people of Judah responded to the Lord's direction. They didn't just do what He said. They *got up early* the next day to fulfill his commands. They gathered in front of the oncoming army. And they "began to sing and praise the Lord" (vv. 20-22). Which sounds to me like they were *acting as if the Lord had already saved them*. That seems important. That's trust.

Are you dying to know what happened? How they made it out of that mess without injury or death? Alright, I'll tell you. The army, which was actually a combination of armies from several lands, began to fight amongst themselves. The infighting among these armies got so bad that they were all slain. All of them. The people of Judah had nothing left to do but go among the dead and collect their spoils. It took them three days to do that. When the work was done, they gathered together again to bless the name of the Lord and give Him their thanks (vv. 24- 26).

There are many scriptural accounts of faithful men and women demonstrating their trust in the Lord, but this one is my favorite. "The battle is not yours but God's." That just gets me every time. We worship a God who is omniscient and omnipotent—all-knowing and all-powerful. Don't you think He might have solutions to our problems that we haven't thought of? Like my siblings on the hiking trail, don't you think His perspective might be broader and more accurate than our own? Couldn't we, maybe, stand still and just trust Him?

Ellie Young, BYU associate professor in the Counseling Psychology and Special Education Department, says this about the importance of trust in our relationship with Jesus Christ: The "safe, trusting relationship that facilitates meaningful growth in counseling is exactly what Christ offers us in a covenant relationship…the Lord promises that He will help us find new ways to move through what is difficult. And because Christ is the expert counselor, He is always understanding, accepting, and willing to listen to our stories again and again."[23]

This trusting relationship comes partly from having a history of experiences with Him. It's likely that you would not open up completely to a new therapist on your first visit. It would take some time, a few visits or more, for trust to develop. Maybe you might cautiously tell your therapist something very personal, just to get her reaction. When she doesn't berate or shame you, you might feel more confident in revealing other aspects of your life.

So it is in our relationship with Christ. We build our trust in Him by receiving, recording and remembering our experiences with Him. We can then say to ourselves, "Well, this is a pretty scary situation. But I remember when I was in x situation and the Lord helped me through it. In fact, I remember some pretty tender mercies He gave me when I was in that hard time. Therefore, I can assume that He will also be there for me now."

The Lord lays this out for us in 2 Nephi 7. The whole chapter is a quote of Isaiah speaking Messianically. Or, in other words, he speaks the words Christ speaks. In this chapter, we are reminded that the Lord has never left us, and that His power to save, heal and help us is never diminished, but we are the ones who are prone to leave Him.

May we learn to say, as He says in the final verses of 2 Nephi 7, "For the Lord God will help me…And the Lord is near, and he justifieth me. Who will contend with me?" (vv. 7-8). May we trust in Him, and never leave Him.

Me-Work: Make a Record

Practice keeping a record of your experiences with the Savior by recording a time when the Lord was there for you. Maybe a time when something that seemed terrible turned out to be good for you.

Here's an example: when I was a young married woman, my husband and I bought a cute little starter home. We loved having our own home and we were in a great ward. We welcomed our first two children into the world while we lived there. Shortly before the first of these two children was born, my husband was suddenly struck with terrible chronic pain that could not be resolved. He fought through it as best he could, but eventually he became unemployed for a time. I had only a part-time job, and soon our financial situation was dire. It looked like we were going to lose our house.

This is the part where I bet you think I'm going to say my husband was healed, or someone paid our mortgage for us for a few months, or I received a lucrative work-at-home job, right? Nope. We lost the house, that cute little house we'd loved so much. It was heart-wrenching, and embarrassing.

So how is this a good example of the Lord being there for me in a hard time? Because, in the complete panic I felt as our foreclosure proceedings loomed, He was there for me. We were a family of four, and we had nowhere to go. Our mortgage was hardly more than apartment rent would be, so if we couldn't afford one, we also couldn't afford the other. One day, the Lord put it into my mind to try to get a job managing a mini storage. I had driven by one and noticed that the office had an apartment attached to it.

This was back in the old days, so I got out the Yellow Pages and called every mini storage in the city. I secured two interviews, which both resulted in job offers. Each came with on-site housing included, and I was able to choose the one that best suited my family's needs.

This was a blessing in three major ways. First, obviously, our housing problem was solved. Second, I could work and take care of my kids in the same space. Third, and maybe most importantly, I was set on a career path that I never would have thought of, and which has blessed my life immensely. From managing the mini-storage, I went on to manage apartments, and then finally to commercial real estate, which I now do from home.

My husband's chronic pain has never been resolved. He sacrifices a lot to work. And when he can't, I've been blessed with a career that allows me to pitch in and keep our family afloat.

Back when we lost our house, I had no way of knowing how badly I would need this long-term career. My plans were to stay home and take care of our babies. I hadn't even finished college! But God knows the end from the beginning. My prayers were to save my house. Instead, He saved my family. I know I can trust Him in any situation.

Can you think of a time when God had your back, even if you didn't realize it in the moment?

_____

_____

_____

_____

_____

_____

_____

_____

_____

_____

_____

_____

_____

_____

_____

_____

Scripture Power

Let's study 2 Kings 6: 14-17

You are probably familiar with the account in 2 Kings of the prophet Elisha in a time of terrible trial, when his city was about to be overrun by Syrians:

14 Therefore sent he thither horses, and chariots, and a great host: and they came by night, and compassed the city about.

15 And when the servant of the man of God was risen early, and gone forth, behold, an host compassed the city both with horses and chariots. And his servant said unto him, Alas, my master! How shall we do?

16 And he answered, Fear not: for they that be with us are more than they that be with them.

17 And Elisha prayed, and said, Lord, I pray thee, open his eyes, that he may see. And the Lord opened the eyes of the young man; and he saw: and, behold, the mountain was full of horses and chariots of fire round about Elisha.

How do you feel as you read this account?

_____

_____

_____

_____

_____

_____

_____

What could you do so that your eyes might be opened to the power
of Christ in your life?

_____

_____

_____

_____

_____

_____

_____

Chapter Four

GOOD CHEER

Part of my job as a manager of commercial real estate is to do some bookkeeping and financial reporting for our clients. I'm competent but not particularly confident in this role. (I'm rarely confident in any role!)

Once, upon taking over a new property, my client emailed me to say his CPA was going to call me to go over a few things.

The Grip hit hard!!! Fear! Distress! Worry! Anxiety! What if he asked me questions I had no idea how to answer? I was sure I was going to end up looking like an idiot. I might even lose this client. The call played out in my mind in various ways, none of them good. I was a nervous wreck.

A couple of days later the call came. After a brief introduction on both sides, here's how the rest of the call went:

CPA: "So, what property management software do you use?"

Me: "Yardi."

CPA: "Hmm, okay. Could you export your financial reports into Excel for me so I can upload them into my software more easily?"

Me: "Sure, no problem."

CPA: "Sounds good, thanks. Bye now."

Me: "Bye."

Yep. That was it. After that phone call was over, I felt both relieved and very, very foolish. Because I know better. I know exactly how anxiety works on me at this point and yet I let it win again. I wish I had given good cheer and optimism a chance instead. What if I had replaced all those worrisome, pretend conversations in my mind with conversations that went well? My mind could suppose, "What if they are calling to ask for my advice because they've heard how amazing I am?" I kind of like that. I could have chosen to *write myself happy*, but I didn't.

Much of anxiety is future-based. We come up with problems that *might* happen, and then we feel anxious because we can't solve them. And we can't solve them because they haven't happened yet. And so we get caught in this downward spiraling vortex of fear. All based on nothing, really. I love this quote from Elder Boyd K. Packer: "You don't tell me worrying doesn't help, because the things I worry about never happen!"[24] That's classic.

A few nights ago (as I write this) my teenage daughter couldn't fall asleep. She was gripped by horrible anxiety, because she had to do a radish project in biology the next day, and the radish seed she was responsible for growing had barely sprouted and wasn't actually a radish yet. She had planted her seed a day or two late and was convinced she was going to fail the project because of it.

The next day when she came home from school, she said, "Oh, guess what? Lots of people in my class had really tiny plants like me."

My sweet girl tortured herself for half the night for absolutely no reason, beating herself up over her perceived shortcomings. We wouldn't treat our worst enemy that way!

Do you ever wonder if God knows how scared we are so very much of the time? I can answer that. He sure does, and here's the proof: what do you do when your small child, niece, nephew or grandchild wakes up in the night with a nightmare? I imagine you hold them close and whisper, "It's okay, little one. Don't be scared. I'm here." That sounds a lot like this: "Fear not, for I have redeemed you. I have called thee by thy name. *Thou art mine*" (Isaiah 43:1, emphasis added). And this, "For I the Lord God will hold thy right hand, saying unto thee, Fear not; I will help thee" (Isaiah 41:13). How about this one? "Wherefore, *be of good cheer*, and do not fear, for I the Lord am with you, and will stand by you" (D&C 68:6, italics added). There are at least a dozen other scriptures with the same message. Our Heavenly Father knew we would be anxious, afraid, and concerned sometimes, and He left us little comforting notes right where we could find them most easily.

I also like this note from Paul, a little piece of his testimony on the subject: "And we know that all things work together for good to them that love God…" (Romans 8:28). Because we know as Paul knows, we can be of good cheer.

"Things don't happen to us, they happen for us." I've heard and read that from such a variety of speakers and bloggers that I don't even know who to credit. I have mixed feelings about this saying, because it feels egotistical to suppose that every event that happens in my life is about me. But here's what I do know for sure—God consistently pulls beauty from ashes. He turns the shape of our sorrows over in His hands until the edges are smoother and parts of it shine with great beauty.

My oldest daughter, Annalyn, had the tremendous opportunity to perform at Carnegie Hall in New York City with the Millennial Choirs and Orchestras (MCO) in the summer of 2019. We traveled there as a family. She was in the Saturday matinee performance, where they sang beautiful songs celebrating both country and Christ. We enjoyed it greatly, and then we went off to get in line for the Broadway show we had tickets for. This was our family's first, and probably only, visit to New York City, so seeing a show was a must and we were all very excited. Well, I'm not sure about my husband, but the rest of us were thrilled.

As we waited in line on the sidewalk of 42nd Street, the power suddenly went off around us. Moments later our phones all beeped. It was a text from Annalyn's conductor. The power was out at Carnegie Hall, too (we later found out we were in the middle of one of the most widespread blackouts the city had ever seen). The conductor asked for our prayers that the power would be restored and the evening concert could proceed as planned.

The concert did, indeed, proceed as planned, just not as MCO had planned. God had a bigger plan, a better one. One in which all those performers had to leave the hall. They then somehow organized themselves out on the street and begin performing there. And then, miraculously, thousands of stranded New Yorkers in the streets and getting air on their balconies listened in as the choir sang a truly heavenly version of *I Stand All Amazed*. Tens of thousands more saw it when a video of the impromptu concert went viral and was picked up by several news agencies.

Most of the people who had tickets to attend that show inside Carnegie Hall were believers, the majority of them family members of the performers. Not so of the audience who filled the streets that night. What an opportunity to spread the message of Christ to some who otherwise might not have heard it. I still get chills remembering that night.

A few days after the blackout I met a woman in the Palmyra temple who lives a few blocks from Carnegie Hall. She was upstate when the blackout happened but told me of the emotional reaction she had when she saw a video of the performance on social media. She explained that she often felt like she couldn't even mention Christ's name in her neighborhood, let alone testify of Him, so to see all those New Yorkers standing silently, listening to song after song about Him—right there on her street? "It made me weep," she said.

Did that blackout happen for me? I sincerely doubt it. I was disappointed to miss our Broadway show, which got cancelled. Many, many children, teens and adults missed out on a once-in-a-lifetime opportunity to perform in Carnegie Hall, and I know they were disappointed as well. I can't even say that I think God orchestrated that blackout. I think the blackout was more likely the result of living in a mortal world, where equipment fails and transformers get overloaded. But *"...even what God does not cause, He can still consecrate."*[25] And boy, did He ever.

I believe our Heavenly Father never misses an opportunity to work good in our lives, and I can tell you that my disappointment at not seeing our Broadway show was totally swallowed up in my joy of seeing those singers testify of Christ on the streets of New York. And this is how all our sorrows, pains and disappointments will feel someday! Whether that blackout started out being for someone or just being a part of life on this earth, I don't know, but it sure ended up being for someone. Doubtless more than one heart was touched on that dark night, including my own.

All these stories are meant to underscore one particular point. We can face our trials, even our anxiety, with good cheer, knowing that beauty somehow comes from ashes when we leave those ashes in our Savior's hands. "The key to access the Savior's enabling power is to submit cheerfully and with patience to the will of the Lord."[26] Just as Alma's people did when they were in bondage to the Lamanites.

The funny thing about Alma's enslaved people is I don't think they got exactly what they wanted from the Lord, not at first. Maybe, just maybe, that's happened to you before. Mosiah 24 doesn't tell us exactly what the people were praying for in their extremity, but being delivered from bondage is a pretty decent guess. And the Lord told them He would deliver them, just not right away. Instead, He made their burdens light while they waited. And Alma's people "did submit cheerfully and with patience to all the will of the Lord" (Mosiah 24:15).

There's so much in that little phrase. So much that so many of us are inherently bad at! Not just submitting to the Lord's will, but doing it cheerfully. Not just accepting his timetable, but doing it patiently. "And it came to pass that so great was their faith and their patience that the voice of the Lord came unto them again, saying: Be of good comfort, for on the morrow I will deliver you out of bondage" (Mosiah 24:16).

Although they submitted to the will of the Lord, it seems to me that Alma's people still exerted some control over their situation. Verse 16 tells me that their faith, patience, submissiveness and good cheer *brought down from heaven* all the blessings the Lord desired to give them.

Submissiveness isn't really an easy idea, is it? But it is key to our happiness. A symbol of our submission to Christ is the yoke, as in "take my yoke upon you" (Matthew 11:28). For a long time, whenever I heard or read that scripture, I would picture the type of yoke that harnesses two oxen together. And I'll be honest, I could never really wrap my mind around that image. I tried to picture myself in that harness, and it never felt comfortable. Even though I knew Christ would be my partner and He would be pulling the load, it felt restrictive to me. I seemed to feel splinters on the back of my neck and a little claustrophobic panic at being trapped in that harness. It just wasn't an image that was working for me, although I recognize it works for others.

I did feel the beauty and importance of the scripture itself, but I needed a better way to understand it. So, I began to study the yoke. I read about farmers who make yokes for their animals by hand. They are made to uniquely fit one particular cow or ox perfectly, so it will be comfortable for them. The farmer spends most of her time working on the curve that goes around the neck, getting it just right and sanding it until it is shiny and smooth—no splinters!

I also learned that yokes aren't just for animals, that there is such a thing as a yoke for humans. And guess what? They don't restrict you or trap you at all. In fact, they are specifically made to lighten loads. They fit over your shoulders and distribute a load, lessening the burden so you can carry it. You've likely seen pictures of women carrying water this way. Now the scripture was starting to make more sense to me. I could read "take my yoke upon you" as Christ saying,

"I see you're carrying a heavy burden. Here, I've spent a lot of time making this yoke just for you. If you accept it from me and use it, it will make your burden lighter and easier to carry. I made it to fit you perfectly and comfortably. It is just what you need."

I liked this new image of a yoke so much that I bought one! It's perfect for object lessons, and I wish you were here with me now so I could demonstrate how much lighter a couple big buckets of water feel when they are balanced on a yoke. We can still choose to carry our water without submitting to the yoke, if we happen to enjoy pain, suffering and spilt water. Why would we choose that?

Remember, life is supposed to be challenging. But hard things need not make us despair, thinking all has gone wrong. We get tripped up in thinking we are supposed to do hard alone. But we were never meant to face our challenges on our own. Confronting hard things, learning, growing, and overcoming—even being temporarily defeated—is God's plan for our eternal success, and He has promised our Savior's help as we do so (see John 14:18). As President Monson has said, "None of us makes it through this life without problems and challenges—and sometimes tragedies and misfortunes. After all, in large part we are here to learn and grow from such events in our lives."[27] Thus, we might understand that if we are experiencing problems and challenges, and especially if we are trying our best to learn and grow from them, then life is actually going just according to plan. His plan. You are doing it right!

That all sounds very practical, but not much fun, right? You might even be asking, tell me again why it's called the plan of happiness? To answer that, we'd have to consider the end game, as Elder Holland helped us do so magnificently when he said, "With the Apostle Paul, I testify that that which was sown in corruption will one day be raised in incorruption and that which was sown in weakness will ultimately be raised in power."[28] We are in the midst of growing from one to the other. From weak to powerful, and into our eternal happiness.

In that process, good cheer can help you have power over anxiety *today*. Keeping in mind the end game, and our Savior's power to get us there if we hearken to Him, can help us realize that *an imperfect life is still a good life*.

There's no better example of good cheer than Sister Marjorie Hinckley. Although she passed away several years ago, she continues to be one of my heroes. I never heard Sister Hinckley give any kind of talk or interview without injecting a good dose of her quiet humor. She never seemed to take her problems too seriously. I remember her saying, "The only way to get through life is to laugh your way through it. You either have to laugh or cry. I prefer to laugh. Crying gives me a headache."[29] If you find good cheer difficult to achieve, study this good lady's life and copy her. I'm sure she won't mind!

Me-Work: Change The Phrase

Negative thinking steals our good cheer. It takes mental energy and practice to remove negative thoughts from our minds. That's what this session of me-work is all about.

Using the space provided, write down a few of the negative things you tell yourself most often, then rewrite them in a positive way. Focus on replacing the negative thoughts with the positive ones each time they come up. If the positive thought is hard to believe at first, feel free to be honest with yourself by adding, "I am working on" or "I believe" in front of the thought. A therapist friend once suggested I think of my brain as a slick, non-stick frying pan and negative thoughts as an egg sliding off the pan. When a negative thought hits me, I bring up that image in my mind of the thought slipping right out, leaving space for me to replace it with a positive.

Example:

Negative – I'm a terrible mom, I just can't seem to keep my kids from fighting.

Opposite Positive – My kids have challenges and so do I, but together we're learning and growing, just like we should be.

_____

_____

_____

_____

_____

_____

_____

_____

_____

_____

_____

Scripture Power

Let's study Psalms 94:19

"In the multitude of my thoughts within me thy comforts delight my soul." I think of this as something like: when my anxious and disquieting thoughts plague me, thoughts of Christ and the care He has given me, the promises He has made to me, and the love I feel from Him bring me joy.

What specific thoughts of Christ's care, promises and love can you turn to again and again?

_____

_____

_____

_____

_____

_____

_____

_____

_____

Chapter Five

FAITH OVER FEAR

I have spent years praying for the gift of faith. I have really taken to heart lessons I have heard about faith and fear like this one: "Fear and faith cannot coexist in our hearts at the same time."[30] I have sometimes felt that I must not be a faithful woman, because I am so often a fearful woman (although I am sure that is not the lesson intended by that quote).

There came a time when I was going through a very personal trial where I had to make some hard decisions. As usual, I turned to my parents and siblings for support, and I kept hearing the same message: "Lecia, you're a woman of great faith and you live close to the Lord. He'll help you figure this out." I wondered how several of the people closest to me could have such a skewed and incorrect image of me. A woman of great faith? No. I was a woman of great fear, especially so during this trial.

Then one morning as I was praying, pleading as usual for faith to replace my fear, I suddenly wondered if maybe *I* had a skewed image of myself. These sudden thoughts or ideas seem to be how the Spirit speaks to me, so I paid attention, and I began to study faith vs. fear.

I was impressed with the idea that I perform many acts of faith every single day, and so do you. I begin and end my day by praying to my Heavenly Father, whom I have never seen in this life, yet I speak to Him as if He were actually there, because I believe He is. Prayer is a pure act of faith.

In my prayers, I repent of the wrongs I've done that day, as if that will somehow make a difference in my life—because I believe that, through Jesus Christ, it makes all the difference. This, too, is an act of faith.

Each time you or I pay tithing, attend the temple, go to church, partake of the sacrament, intentionally try to keep a commandment, or do any number of other things, we are demonstrating faith.

Imagine what the truly faithless life really looks like. Imagine how you might behave every day if you believed that we, along with all our loved ones, ended up as living organisms on the earth by pure accident, that there is no purpose to being here, and that we cease to exist upon death. Would your life look different if this were what you truly believed? Would you pray? Would you care about repentance? Would you go to the temple? Why would you? There would be no point.

Here's what I learned through my studies. Faith and fear cannot coexist in the same heart at the same time, but they can switch out with each other quickly and frequently. I think that must be how it is with me. And that's okay. Over time, I hope the moments I have faith in my heart will outnumber the moments I have fear in greater and greater proportions. I believe that will happen!

You and I are far more faithful than we ever imagined.

And by the way, let's make sure we're clear on something— fear and anxiety are normal human emotions, not sins.[31] Everybody experiences these emotions in differing degrees and circumstances. You are on your path. It includes anxiety. That's okay. Your path still leads home, it still leads to Him.

Feeling fear doesn't mean we're not worthy or that we're useless to the Lord because our faith isn't strong enough. Want an example of someone who feared and also served God with great faith? Let's talk about Gideon.

Gideon lived in some rather extraordinary circumstances, dangerous circumstances even. And Gideon was often afraid. And yet the Lord used him in some rather extraordinary ways. During the time his account takes place, as recorded in Judges chapters 6 and 7, the children of Israel were in bondage to the Midianites. To make matters worse, the Midianites had destroyed Israel's crops and herds of cattle, so they were in great need, likely close to starvation.

In Judges 6:11 Gideon is threshing wheat behind the winepress, trying to hide what he's doing from the Midianites. I'm guessing if his captors discovered him, they would take his food for themselves.

As he's threshing, an angel of the Lord appears to him, and greets Gideon by saying, "The Lord is with thee, thou mighty man of valour."

Just to be clear, valour (noun) = boldness or determination in facing great danger, especially in battle; heroic courage; bravery.

How would you react if an angel came and hailed you as mighty, brave and courageous? I think I would shake my head no. Not me. You've got me confused with someone else.

Gideon is in that same head space, apparently. First, he questions whether the Lord is really with him. He says, basically, if the Lord is with us, then why are we in this horrible situation? It seems more accurate to say the Lord has forsaken us.

The angel becomes more clear with him and says, "Go in this thy might, and thou shalt save Israel from the Midianites: have I not sent thee?"

And here it is, the disbelief. Gideon shakes his head, no. Not me. You're confusing me with someone else. His actual words are, "... wherewith shall I save Israel? Behold, my family is poor in Manasseh, and I am the least in my father's house."

The angel continues to insist that Gideon is the man the Lord has chosen for the job, and that the Lord will attend him in this great errand.

Gideon then proceeds to ask for a sign that all this is true. And he doesn't just ask for a sign once. He doesn't just ask twice. Three times he asks for a sign, and each time he is given what he asks for.

Could anything be more comforting to someone suffering from anxiety than to read this account of the infinite patience of the Lord? The Lord saw Gideon's doubt and fear and He patiently stood with him as he worked through it. Never once did He say, "Forget it, you're really not cut out for this job. I'll find someone less anxious and more perfect than you."

Never think that having anxiety means the Lord can't use you. *He has always known you.* He, better than anyone, knows your temperament, your strengths and your weaknesses. The purposes he has set for you to accomplish were set with those traits already in mind. Whatever it is He asks you to do, He already knows you can do it, and He will stand patiently with you as you work to come to that conclusion for yourself. Gideon had to work through his own doubts and fears before he could tackle the job the Lord had given him. Note, though, that he worked through them *with the Lord.*

So it comes to pass that Gideon amasses an army to fight the Midianites, but the Lord wants to make sure Israel knows Who has delivered them. In order to prevent them from boasting in their own strength, the Lord tells Gideon to whittle down the size of his army, which he does, twice.

The first time the Lord has Gideon shrink the size of his army, He tells Gideon to simply ask, "Who's afraid?" And whoever is afraid is allowed to leave the army and return home. Guess how many of these big, bad warriors admitted to being afraid? Out of 32,000 soldiers, 22,000 of them turned and went home! Did I mention already that fear is a rather normal human emotion?

The Lord then whittles the army down again, to just 300, and tells Gideon the time has come for him to save Israel against the mighty and numerous armies of the Midianites. Here's my favorite part. The part that proves we worship a God who understands us, who knows we have fears and weaknesses. The Lord says to Gideon, "Arise, get thee down unto the host; for I have delivered it unto thine hand. But if thou fear to go down, go thou with Phurah thy servant… and *afterward* shall thine hands be strengthened to go down unto the host."

Gideon, now, has had more than one conversation with the Lord and an angel of the Lord. Gideon has received three miraculous signs from the Lord. So what does he do at this point? He "went down *with Phurah* his servant…" I just love that whole thing. The Lord acknowledges that, despite his many witnesses, Gideon might still be afraid, and He makes an allowance for that.

And Gideon, mighty Gideon, does what the Lord asks him to do, *in spite of his fear.* And *then,* after his obedience, his hand is strengthened. He's given the strategy he needs to defeat the Midianites, and the children of Israel are delivered from their bondage.

The Lord doesn't want us to fear, but He does stand by us when we do. Many, many times in the scriptures He, or one of His servants, reminds us that we need not fear. These scriptures are worth a careful study. I'll list a few of the references here, and I invite you to take the time to look at them closely. As you read, ask yourself, what situation caused the Lord to issue the command to fear not? How did the person being spoken to respond? What changed after that? Ask yourself how you could respond in similar situations.

Genesis 26:24	Numbers 14:9	2 Kings 6:16
Isaiah 51:7	Matthew 1:20	Matthew 28:5
Revelation 1:17	D&C 6:33	D&C 38:15, 30
D&C 136:17	D&C 67:10	D&C 98:1

Notes:

_____

_____

_____

_____

_____

_____

_____

_____

_____

_____

_____

_____

_____

_____

_____

_____

When I began to study fear and anxiety, one of the harder truths I had to swallow is that fear can be an offspring of pride. I didn't think pride was one of my weaknesses, but the more I learned about this aspect of anxiety, the more I realized how wrong I was. Consider President Benson's comment, "(Pride) is the fear of man over the fear of God."[32] And this from D&C 3:7-8, "For behold, you should not have feared man more than God. Although men set at naught the counsels of God, and despise his words – yet you should have been faithful; and he would have extended his arm and supported you against all the fiery darts of the adversary; and he would have been with you in every time of trouble."

I have to admit that many of my fears and anxieties are "others" based. I worry about the rude remark one of my children makes at a family gathering because others might judge me to be a bad mom. I stress over making a mistake at work because I've displayed my imperfections to others. I'm anxious about a talk I'm going to give because I want others to love it and to love me when I'm done giving it. These are just a few examples of classic anxieties based on the fear of man. They are also all very self-focused thoughts. Prideful, even. Having a self-centered agenda for everything we do and say is a great way to grow and enhance anxiety in our lives.

The opposite of this, of course, is to become other-centered, to focus our lives on serving God and His children. President Gordon B. Hinckley said it very clearly, "The antidote of selfishness is service, a reaching out to those about us—those in the home and those beyond the walls of the home."[33] Here we have the classic mathematical property, if A = B and B = C then A = C. In this case, if service is the antidote to selfishness (self-focus), and *self-focus breeds and magnifies anxiety*, then it stands to reason that service is also an antidote for anxiety.

It seems that service comes up in conference talks, church magazine articles, and gospel lessons as the antidote to a lot of things, including anxiety, depression, loneliness, physical pain, and other heavy trials. But if you feel the urge to bemoan the near constant repetition of this principle, instead ask yourself why. Why is it mentioned so many times? What is the power of service? Could it really help? Ponder on it a bit, and then experiment on the word. Give it a try. Get invested in a cause outside your own well-being and see what happens.

You see, serving is an action. And action beats anxiety over the head! Anxiety can be paralyzing, bringing us to a standstill. BYU professor Gregory Clark asked a pointed question in a devotional he gave at the university: what is the source of fear? His answer seems spot-on to me. "I think it is rooted in the assumption...that I must solve all my problems and face all my challenges alone, using my own resources. That is frightening, because deep in my heart I know how limited those resources are. So, when I am fearful, I am also hopeless. And without hope, I find myself paralyzed. Knowing that I am not capable of changing myself or my circumstances for the better, I stand frozen in fear."[34]

The only real solution to that paralyzing anxiety is to unfreeze yourself by taking action. To give service, for example, or to try something even though you're scared to do so. Why does this work? Because by taking action, you displace your fear with faith. Action is a manifestation of faith! As James teaches us in the Bible, "Even so faith, if it hath not works, is dead, being alone" (James 2:17). When you move forward in the face of fear, you are exercising faith that things will turn out okay. That what you do matters. That your actions will amount to something. You are also choosing, by your action, to nourish faith over fear.

You know this is true because it has played out in your life, as it has in mine, over and over. Think about stressing over a low bank balance. There's only one thing that can make you feel better when you have no money, and that is to figure out a way to make some money, and then go do it. Or think about the last time you had to study for a big test. You might have felt overwhelmed (a common precursor to anxiety) with the amount of information you had to memorize. So you put off the studying. You did everything else you could possibly do except study. You did the dishes, watched Netflix, made a snack, called a friend. You might have even paid bills if you were truly desperate. None of those distractions made you feel better, though. Now remember how it felt when you finally sat down and cracked open that book. It felt like opening the release on a pressure valve, right? The anxiety finally had a chance to seep out. *It feels good to take faithful action when we feel fear.*

The most important action we can take is to turn to Christ in our paralyzing anxiety. Remember the disciples of Christ who, in the midst of a fierce storm and some pretty powerful fear, woke their sleeping Master and cried, "Master, carest thou not that we perish?" (Mark 4:38).

It gives me some comfort that these disciples, who literally walked with Jesus and had seen Him perform many miracles, still felt fear.

Brother Clark notes this important point, "Founded upon promises of the past and the future, our faith can be vulnerable when experiences in the present seem to contradict both. So even with knowledge of the truth, in the present moments of our day-to-day experience we remain subject to fear and must consciously choose again and again to believe, to remember, to hope, to have faith." For a time, the disciples' present troubles—the fierce storm—outweighed their faith. Yet, they knew to Whom they should run. Their fear motivated them to turn to Christ, as it should us. That's godly anxiety.

In the end, I do believe that faith and fear cannot coexist. Instead of making you feel hopeless, I want that thought to make you very, very happy, because it means that you are in control. You are a faithful daughter or son of God. You manifest that faith in dozens of small ways each and every day. Thus, you have the power to drive anxiety and fear away, even if only for a moment. You do that by taking action, perhaps by reading and remembering Christ's promises to stand by us, or by doing something that is completely other-centered. Then a moment later, you can do it again.

Me-Work: Practice

This me-work is all about a few practical actions you can take when feeling anxious. Look them over, and circle one or two that might help you, then practice using them this week.

Tip #1: Remember that fear is basically a survival instinct, built into us to keep us safe. This means that, in some circumstances, it's a useful tool. For example, our instinct to stay in well-lit areas when walking alone at night is a useful manifestation of anxiety. But most of the time we feel fear, we are not in any actual danger. We just have to train our brain to realize that.

When the Grip hits, ask yourself, am I actually in danger right now? When the answer is no (as it usually will be), go ahead and move forward, even if you have to do it scared. *Say out loud to yourself, "I am not in danger here."*

Tip #2: A common form of anxiety is self-doubt. As in, "What was I thinking? I can't do this!" Or, "Everyone else is better at this than me!" Or, "I can't cook dinner for the missionaries, they'll hate anything I make!" This is your anxiety trying to inform the future. You don't know how things will turn out, but you're acting like you do.

Imagine you just put in for a promotion at work. Your thoughts might immediately go to, "Why did I do that? Cheryl put in for the promotion, too, and she's way more qualified than me. She'll get the promotion, and everyone will know I got beat out. It will be so humiliating!" This is your brain trying to protect you, when instead it's actually damaging you, creating failure that hasn't happened yet.

However, *if we recognize that pattern, we can change it.* Instead of running down a negative road when you feel this kind of anxiety, it's helpful to say something neutral about the situation, such as, "Well, this is interesting." Or, "I can't wait to see how this turns out!" This reminds your brain that you don't yet know the outcome. And guess what? It could be good!

Tip #3: Anxiety is often past- or future-based. You remember that you failed at something in the past. You remember that you haven't been perfect. Or, your mind predicts a dire future ahead.

When you're stuck in past- or future-based anxiety, try to ground yourself in the present by focusing on what's real, right now. Think about each of your senses and what they are experiencing in this moment: I feel a breeze on my face. I smell tacos. I hear my kids giggling (or fighting, let's be real). Checking in with your senses checks you back into the present, where you are safe and well, and have so much to be grateful for.

Tip #4: There is opposition in *all* things (see 2 Nephi 2:11). There is an opposite of all things. For every negative, fear-filled thought your mind can come up with, there is an equal but opposite positive thought. Try replacing one with the other. For example, if you like to tell yourself, "I'm never going to be able to go back to school," you could replace that with, "I don't know how right now, but I know I can get back into school." If your mind tells you that your idea is stupid and people will laugh, you could tell yourself instead that your idea is unique, and people will love it. Either outcome is equally probable, so why feed yourself the negative one every day?

Tip #5: Try living with your anxiety rather than fighting it. Just don't let it own you. I love the metaphor author Elizabeth Gilbert uses in her book *Big Magic: Creative Living Beyond Fear*. Speaking to her fear, she says, "There's plenty of room in this vehicle for all of us, so make yourself at home, but understand this: Creativity and I are the only ones who will be making any decisions along the way. I recognize and respect that you are part of this family, and so I will never exclude you from our activities, but still—your suggestions will never be followed. You're allowed to have a seat, and you're allowed to have a voice, but you are not allowed to have a vote." *Never allow anxiety to take over the Spirit's job of guiding your decisions.*

Tip #6: We jokingly call this one the "Law of Lecia" at my house because it's useful in so many situations that I say it often: the body is easier to control than the mind. Therefore, if you find yourself overwhelmed with anxious thoughts and are having a hard time redirecting them, try moving your body instead. Get up and do 20 jumping jacks; give your kid a fun piggyback ride; sing a song while you cook something. When you move your body, your mind naturally gets pushed off the one-track thinking it was stuck on.

Which tip(s) will you commit to practicing this week?

_____

_____

_____

_____

_____

_____

_____

_____

Scripture Power

Let's study Hebrews 2:15
"And deliver them who through fear of death
were all their lifetime subject to bondage."

In this scripture, Paul is hoping to give Christ's followers a new and better perspective, just as my mom and sisters did for me when they helped me to stop seeing myself as a faithless woman. Paul wanted his readers to stop fearing death and look at it from a new perspective, that of a promised resurrection through Christ.

What fears do you have that are keeping you in bondage? What might be a different perspective?

_____

_____

_____

_____

_____

_____

_____

_____

_____

_____

Chapter Six

LOVE

"Your friend from high school told a story about you in Relief Society today," my mom said one day as I visited with her. Mom told me the woman's name, but I didn't recognize it. Of course, since I graduated from high school...well, more than a few years ago, I can't be expected to remember everyone I knew back then, right?

This classmate had related a story in Relief Society of a day when she had been sitting in the hallway of the seminary building one day, feeling down. "And your daughter," she said, pointing to my mom, "sat down beside me and asked if I was okay."

Not a big deal, I know. But somehow, that small moment of connection between the two of us meant enough to her that she still remembered it all these years later.

I don't remember the incident at all.

But I've thought about it often since my mom relayed that story to me. I did a lot of stupid things in high school, and there were times when I was incredibly thoughtless. Once I wrote a note to a friend saying that I was getting tired of this one particular girl who hung around with me. And then the girl I was complaining about SAW my note. I was genuinely horrified by what I'd done and apologized profusely, and she was gracious enough to forgive me. But guess what?

I remember every detail of *that* incident, even though it's also decades in the past. I remember the room I was sitting in when I passed the note. I remember the look on the other girl's face when she saw what I had written. I feel sick writing about it now, because I remember all of it, and many other incidents where I made similar or worse mistakes.

These scenes like to replay themselves in my mind every now and then. But here's the thing. The girl who wrote the unkind note and the girl who took time to talk to someone in the hallway were the same girl. They were both me. But when I remember my 17-year-old self, I can only seem to remember the part of me who wrote the unkind note and did a hundred other stupid things.

I bet I did a hundred other nice things, too (at least, I desperately hope I did), but our minds can be like that. They are super glue for negative memories and a slip-n-slide for positive ones. I believe I've let a whole half of my 17-year-old self slip-n-slide right into oblivion.

Which means I can't ever really reminisce about the past because it gives me anxiety. I'm on the outs with my past self, and boy! One sure way to increase anxiety is to have a rift with someone, *especially if that person is you.*

Jesus Christ must have surely had our mental health in mind when He gave us the two great commandments. "Thou shalt love the Lord thy God with all thy heart, and with all thy soul, and with all thy mind" and "Thou shalt love thy neighbor as thyself" (Matthew 22:37,39). It is of the utmost importance to Christ that we love God, our neighbors, and *ourselves*. In fact, He's also famously commanded us to love our enemies (see Matthew 5:44). What is it about love that makes it so supremely central to the great commandments?

Well, for one thing, so much relief from anxiety comes from love. President Dieter F. Uchtdorf said, "I pray with all the strength of my soul that we may become liberated from this fear by the divinely appointed antidote to fear: the pure love of Christ, for 'perfect love casteth out fear.'"[35]

Let's dig into the rich subject of perfect love and how it can help us manage anxiety by starting with 1 John 4:12. "If we love one another, God dwelleth in us, and his love is perfected in us." In other words, "If we love one another, God continues in union with us, and His love in all its perfection is in our hearts" (Weymouth New Translation). *His* perfect love dwells in us.

Verse 16 continues, "...he that dwelleth in love dwelleth in God, and God in him," and then we return again to, "perfect love casteth out all fear."

Let's recap: Perfect love can cast out fear. Think of adding pretty pebbles to a jar of water and watching the water rise and then spill out of the jar as the pebbles displace it. The more our souls are filled with the love of Christ, the less room there is for fear. Thankfully, perfect love is not us being perfect at loving everyone and everything. Instead, perfect love is *HIS* love, the pure love of Christ. That perfect love can dwell in us.

"The deepest love comes when we are one with God."[36]

Return to our imagery of walking with Christ from Chapter Two. Being one with God means following our Savior and doing what He does, for He is one with His Father (John 10:30. It's keeping our covenant to always remember Him. It's giving the soft answer (Proverbs 15:1), turning the other cheek (Matthew 5:39), and praying for those who wrong us (Matthew 5:44).

It's crying with our friends when they are hurting, even if their hurt has been self-inflicted through poor choices (Mosiah 18:9). Maybe especially then, when others will surely abandon them.

Being one with God means walking the difficult path beside someone, lifting them when they stumble[37], even though our own path feels dreadfully difficult itself.

It is following Christ.

Rich treasures await us when we live with God's perfect love in our hearts: "Love covereth all sins," (Proverbs 10:12). This scripture is frequently misunderstood to mean that we need not worry about sinning so long as we express our devotion to Christ. But Jesus Christ himself corrects this misinterpretation when he says, "If ye love me, keep my commandments," (John 14:15), not, "If you just love me, then you can sin as much as you want."

There are several other, more meaningful ways to interpret this scripture. Such as, when you are full of the love of Christ, you are better able to overlook the sins of others. What a great blessing! Also, the Atonement of Christ is a gift of pure love which covers all sins.

When we are filled with charity, we lose the desire to sin, as charity is everlastingly kind, long-suffering and merciful (see 1 Corinthians 13). This state of being would indeed be a rich treasure.

Perhaps it could also mean that, as we are filled with God's love, we become better at loving ourselves and thus more capable of forgiving ourselves for the wrongs we have done.

Few things induce more anxiety than being at odds with another human being. Nothing brings on The Grip quite like having a falling-out with a friend or family member. Maybe God's injunction to love our enemies (Matthew 5:44) is His loving way of relieving us from the huge anxiety that comes from having enemies at all. It also serves as a reminder that love is central to all our relationships, including the one we have with ourselves.

Living in love brings peace. For those of us afflicted with anxiety this is a true gift indeed. Christ himself tells us of the peace love brings in a revelation he gave to Joseph Smith now known as Section 88 of the Doctrine & Covenants. Joseph called this section "the Lord's message of peace to us," and in it, He says: "Above all things, clothe yourselves with the bond of charity, as with a mantle, which is the bond of perfectness and peace" (vs. 125). A mantle is a cloak, worn over the other layers of clothing, protecting them from the weather and providing the wearer with a layer of warmth. Imagine the pure love of Christ covering you like a cloak of peace and healing.

Did you know love is also part of the armor of God? Part of the protection we should always be wearing? Love is the breastplate (see 1 Thessalonians 5:8), that piece of armor that covers many of the most vital organs of the body, making love essential to our well-being and safety.

How do we cultivate this kind of love within ourselves? "We earnestly reach for Heavenly Father's help, in the name of His Son, and do things His way instead of pridefully asserting our own will."[38] We cannot be filled with the love of Christ if we are not in unity with Him. Imagine your unity with Christ as a conduit, allowing His love to flow unfettered into your heart.

"We want to be encircled in the arms of our Heavenly Father's love and guidance, and so we put His will first and with a broken heart plead that Christ will pour streams of cleansing water into our pitcher. At first it may come drop by drop, but as we seek, ask, and obey, it will come abundantly. This living water will begin to fill us, and brimming with His love, we can tip the pitcher of our soul and share its contents with others who thirst for healing, hope, and belonging."[39]

When we submit our will to God's, we follow Christ's example of being in perfect union with His Father. This allowed Him to love as the Father loves. "If ye keep my commandments, ye shall abide in my love; even as I have kept my Father's commandments, and abide in his love" (John 15:10).

Perhaps the best way to gain greater capacity to love others, the second great commandment, is to follow the first great commandment and love God with all our hearts, meaning that our greatest desire is to keep His commandments. When we do, He (and His perfect love) can dwell in us, and we in Him (see John 17:21). Remember, the more our souls are filled with His love, the less room there is for fear.

Jesus Christ demonstrated His perfect love for the Father and for us through His willingness to sacrifice for our sakes. Sacrifice and service are the helpmeets of love: sacrifice and service grow our love; love grows our desire to sacrifice and serve.

At the age of 14, one of my daughters was in that "Mom is an idiot" stage. That's not a fun stage! I was praying it would end soon, and it did, but not in the way I expected. My daughter had a small accident, and her arm was immobile for a couple of weeks. Because of this, she required a lot more service from me than a 14-year-old normally would, the most memorable being my efforts to reach around the shower curtain and wash her hair while still maintaining some semblance of privacy for her. There was something magical and heart-softening about this service, and by the time her arm was healed, so was our relationship. *Love blooms in an atmosphere of sacrifice.*

Finally, I will say from personal experience that it is far easier to focus on love when we are not focused on ourselves. However, looking outward is most easily done when we feel secure, and those who struggle with anxiety rarely feel secure. If insecurity makes it hard for you to love and serve, please revisit Chapter Three, where we learned about trust together. The greatest form of security is the knowledge that Christ has you. He's got your back, He has you covered, He's always there. When you trust Christ implicitly, your power to love will blossom.

Me-Work

Write the name of someone you love and admire (even if it's from afar). Then write 5-10 traits this person has that make them so admirable.

_____

_____

_____

_____

Now go back and cross off the name of the person you wrote and write your name instead. Read through the list of traits you listed and believe that those traits belong to you as well. Often, the traits we admire so in other people are the very traits lying in vast reservoirs, perhaps undetected, in ourselves. Did you know—someone may be writing about YOU as their me-work right now. *YOU* are admirable. *YOU* are supremely loveable. YOU ARE LOVED.

Scripture Power

Let's study 1 John 4:13-16

13 Hereby know we that we dwell in him, and he in us, because he hath given us of his Spirit.

14 And we have seen and do testify that the Father sent the Son *to be* the Saviour of the world.

15 Whosoever shall confess that Jesus is the Son of God, God dwelleth in him, and he in God.

16 And we have known and believed the love that God hath to us. God is love; and he that dwelleth in love dwelleth in God, and God in him.

How would you summarize these verses? What message is there for you personally? Think of how you feel when the Spirit is present. Think of the sacrifice it took for our Parents in heaven to give their eldest son to the world, out of love for us. Think of actually having Someone in your life who loves you so fully, so comprehensively, that He *is* love. What would it mean to share a dwelling place with Someone like that?

_____

_____

Chapter Seven

REPENTANCE

Nothing compares to the pressure of being in the final stages of a spelling bee, even if it's just the fourth-grade bee and not the Scripps National. I never won a spelling bee when I was young, although I vaguely remember coming close (did I spell vaguely right?).

My mom, who at the time of this writing is 79 years old, has forgotten a few things from her life. But one thing she will never forget is her elementary school spelling bee. She didn't win, and it still bothers her, mainly because she knew how to spell the word that got her out. She just flubbed it for some reason. The fact that she made a mistake just eats at her. Ironically, the word she flubbed was "guilty." Anytime the subject of spelling or spelling bees comes up, my poor mom gets all squirmy and uncomfortable, and inevitably she has to spell out g-u-i-l-t-y just to prove she can do it.

This story reminds me of how I feel when I make a mistake. Squirmy and uncomfortable might be the best of the feelings that descend on me when I've done wrong, whether willfully or unintentionally. Unless you're one of those rare people whose every moment is Instagram-worthy, I'm guessing you know what I mean. (Don't try to tell me those perfect people don't exist—my feed is full of them!)

I'm one of those weird people who loves the Bible Dictionary. If you are ever studying a topic for any reason, don't forget to check the Bible Dictionary, there is some great stuff in there. Here's what the Bible Dictionary says about fear, and when I read it for the first time it just about struck me down: "The first effect of Adam's sin was that he was afraid." It cites Genesis 3:10, but I'm telling you, I never latched on to that, and I went to seminary and I attend the temple and everything. Here is the verse in its entirety: "And he (Adam) said, I heard thy voice in the garden, and I was afraid, because I was naked; and I hid myself."

Adam had transgressed, thus opening himself up to the influence of Satan. And what did Satan tell him? To be afraid! And to hide his sin.

This is the origin story of a pattern that has repeated itself ad nauseum throughout history. Transgression or sin, that is, unresolved sin, opens us up to the influence of Satan. And Satan tells us to be afraid. To hide our mistakes. To pretend we're perfect and haven't done anything wrong. In other words, unresolved sin gives Satan power to influence us, thus making us miserable like himself (2 Nephi 2:27). These messages of fear would never come from God, they are not in keeping with His perfect character.

So, sometimes when we think we are feeling anxiety, we are actually feeling guilt, or remorse, or shame, or maybe all of the above. If those feelings become the godly sorrow that moves us to repentance (see 2 Cor 7:10), then this kind of fear can turn to our good. If not, it eats away at us endlessly. The Bible Dictionary continues with its definition of fear: "Sin destroys that feeling of confidence God's child should feel in a loving Father and produces instead a feeling of shame and guilt. *Ever since the Fall God has been teaching men not to fear, but with penitence to ask forgiveness in full confidence of receiving it.*"

Fear often keeps people from repenting, and it has done so for me in the past. I remember making a big, HUGE mistake in my first "real" job, an actual office job, when I was about twenty-one. I worked as a secretary in a tax firm, and one day I mistakenly shredded a client's W-2s!

My boss was not an understanding kind of guy (he once threw a stapler at me), and I'll never forget the fear that gripped my heart when I realized what I had done, or how frantically I tried to come up with ways to fix my mistake without having to confess to either my boss or our client. It felt like the very most important thing in the world that nobody find out what had happened. Without realizing it, I was under the influence of Satan. I was fearful and focused on hiding, and that made for a couple of truly miserable days.

I'd like to say I finally 'fessed up in full honesty and all was well, but I think what actually happened is I found another copy of the W-2 in the client's file, called the IRS to see if a photocopy was acceptable, and actually managed to resolve the issue without confessing. But I'll never forget how awful I felt.

Now when I make a mistake at work or at home, I try to remember to take a deep breath, admit what I've done, offer possible solutions, and promise to do better in the future. It hurts for a moment, but the moment passes quickly and without subjecting me to Satan's persistent influence.

Now when I have done wrong and least feel like praying because I want to hide my face from God, I know that it's imperative that I get on my knees right then. And guess what? He has never, ever turned me away.

Is there anything more miserable than delaying repentance? I love how Sister Carolyn J. Rasmus approaches the topic of repentance in her talk, "Our Savior's Love."[40] She tells of a time when she was driving to a speaking engagement, and realized she had made a wrong turn. Sister Rasmus didn't debate about whether to keep moving in the wrong direction or turn around and get back on track. Of course she turned around!

And so should you and I. Why do we debate whether or not we should get back on track when we've done wrong? Why do we continue in the wrong direction when we know it's not leading us anywhere good? Usually, the answer is fear. Fear of confessing. Fear of the judgments of others. Fear that what we've broken can't be fixed. Fear that *we* can't be fixed.

None of those fears come from God. As Elder James Rasband so movingly reminded us, *"...the Savior will mend all that we have broken. And He will also mend us if we turn to Him in faith and repent of the harm we have caused."*[41]

Certainly, we cannot resolve anxiety over sin without Christ.

My parents once sent the gift of a book to a relative, and within its pages they slid a $100 bill, a very generous sum as they raised their large family. They never heard from this relative about either the book or the surprise it contained, so they were left to assume the book went unopened and the gift unspent.

This is the sort of ungratefulness we display to our precious Savior and Redeemer when we leave the gift of His Atonement, given at such a high price, unopened by refusing to turn our sins over to Him through repentance. Hiding and justifying our sins hurts not only us, but must surely hurt Him as well.

But what if you have sincerely repented and still can't stop thinking anxiously about past sins? Or even just innocent mistakes? I know many of us are almost used to feeling our hearts and guts clench with anxiety when a random trigger brings to mind a thoughtless remark or deed from as far back as elementary school.

In fact, yellow school buses still remind me of the time when, as a shy 8-year-old, I failed to stand up to some older boys who were making fun of another kid on the bus. Logically, I understand that God is surely not holding that moment against me, but my ever-loyal companion the Grip likes to tell me otherwise.

The words of Elder Richard G. Scott provide good perspective in situations like this. "To you who have sincerely repented yet continue to feel the burden of guilt, realize that to continue to suffer for sins when there has been proper repentance and forgiveness of the

Lord is prompted by the master of deceit. Lucifer will encourage you to continue to relive the details of past mistakes, knowing that such thoughts can hamper your progress. Thus, he attempts to tie strings to the mind and body so that he can manipulate you like a puppet to discourage personal achievement."[42]

I really DO NOT want to be Satan's puppet, and so I must recognize that beating myself up over sins that have been cleared with the Lord is playing right into Satan's hands. It prevents growth, and in the Lord's plan, growth must be. "But this one thing I do, forgetting those things that are behind, and reaching forth unto those things which are before, I press forward toward the mark for the prize of the high calling of God in Christ Jesus" (Philippians 3:13-14).

Remember that "If you are trying to pay for your sins" through your own efforts, misery, self-flagellation, etc., "understand that you are missing the very essence of God's plan for you. The Savior has paid the price already. Only Satan wants you to think you can't be forgiven and that you have to pay for your own sins. Let them go and do it today. Your daily happiness comes as you free yourself from thinking and worrying about your past sins…"[43]

I'd like to give you a new perspective on what it means to be somebody who has had to repent. Somebody who messes up, makes mistakes, maybe quite regularly. Someone like me, in other words! Sister Sharon Eubank gave me this perspective in a single sentence. This statement of hers completely floored me and, really, allowed me to love myself again. Let me say first, Sister Eubank is a champion of repentance. Study her talks and you will find that thread woven everywhere. Her sentence that meant so much to me was this: "Women who have repented change the course of history."[44] And of course that goes for men, too. This statement of hers opened my eyes. Instead of seeing myself as a sinner who had disappointed God, I began to see myself as a repenter who could thus serve God, "armed with righteousness, and the power of God in great glory (1 Nephi 14:14). As Nelson Mandela said, "Saints are sinners who keep on trying."[45] Can you think of 'trying' as a synonym for 'repenting'? *Saints are sinners who keep on repenting.* Doesn't that ring true inside the part of you that is ancient, and eternal, and wise?

I am a child of God who has repented and continues to do so. I'm guessing you are, too. But perhaps you are having some serious doubts right now about whether you have ever, or could ever, change the course of history?

A while back I decided I was going to switch all the outdoor light bulbs on my house from incandescent to LED. One night, I went outside with a sleeve of LED bulbs in my hand to make the change. I turned all the lights off, replaced one bulb, then turned the lights back on to make sure the bulb worked. I was immediately struck by the difference the bulb made in that corner of my house. By comparison, the areas with the regular bulbs looked dim and yellowish. The new bulb burned bright and clean. I quickly realized I would need to sweep my house free of cobwebs and dirt if I were going to follow through on my plan to change all the bulbs. Changing that one bulb was a real eye-opener.

And so it is with us. We change one heart—our own—through the cleansing power of Christ's Atonement, and suddenly we see new possibilities. We reach out and gently dust the cobwebs off another's heart, and their light begins to shine a little brighter, too.

This is how repentant women and men change history. *When we are no longer weighed down by our sins, our eyes clear and we see what we haven't before. Then we can do what we couldn't before.*

If there is any repentance you have been putting off, I invite you to take care of it today. If there is any already-repented-of sin that you continue to beat yourself up about, I invite you to believe that when Christ says He has cleansed you, He has. That sin is gone, as completely as if it never happened. "Behold, he who has repented of his sins, the same is forgiven, and I, the Lord, remember them no more," (D&C 58:42).

Sister Linda S. Reeves gives a touching account that illustrates this point. "A few months before President Boyd K. Packer passed away, general priesthood and auxiliary leaders had the precious opportunity of having him speak to us. I have not been able to quit thinking about what he said. He shared that he had searched backward throughout his lifetime, looking for evidence of the sins that he had committed and sincerely repented of, and he could find *no trace* of them. Because of the atoning sacrifice of our beloved Savior, Jesus Christ, and through sincere repentance, his sins were completely gone, as if they had never happened. President Packer then charged us as leaders that day to testify that this is true for each one of us who sincerely repents."[46]

Me-Work: Forward, Not Back

Have the courage to repent, and the courage to forgive yourself. Consider memorizing this quote by Ralph Waldo Emerson and repeating it whenever you're tempted to dwell on past mistakes.

"Finish each day and be done with it. You have done what you could. Some blunders and absurdities no doubt crept in; forget them as soon as you can. Tomorrow is a new day. You shall begin it serenely and with too high a spirit to be encumbered with your old nonsense."

Scripture Power

Let's study Philippians 3:13-14.

13 Brethren, I count not myself to have apprehended: but this
   one thing I do, forgetting those things which are behind,
   and reaching forth unto those things which are before
14 I press toward the mark, for the prize of the high calling of

   God in Christ Jesus.

Paul is certain of one thing he must do: forget things that are
_____ him and look toward things that are _____,
particularly his eternal victory with Christ Jesus.

What do you worry about that likely will not matter in a year?

_____

_____

_____

What do you worry about that likely will not matter in 5 years?

_____

_____

_____

What do you worry about that won't matter in the eternities?

_____

_____

_____

Anything that's still on your list after those 3 filters, turn over to
your Father in Heaven. You worship a God who can handle it.

Conclusion

I've made quite a few confessions in this book, but have I admitted to you yet that I wear contact lenses? Yep, I wear them. Since 5th grade, in fact.

It's kind of embarrassing, right? I mean, I should probably be able to figure this vision thing out on my own, or pray with enough faith to be healed, but instead I've worn contacts for many years. Only a few of my friends wear contacts, at least that I know of. Maybe more do and have just never admitted it, I don't know. It's not like it's something we would just open up about. I'm afraid there might be something really wrong with me.

Okay, stop! I'm sure you realize how silly that sounds. But let's replace "contacts" with "anxiety medication" and see if it sounds a little more familiar.

I have anxiety, and I take medication for it. It's kind of embarrassing. I feel like I should be able to figure out how to get out of my own head, or have enough faith to just stop worrying, but that hasn't happened. I'm not sure any of my friends are dealing with this. At least, if they are, it doesn't come up in conversation. It's not really something we would talk about. I feel like everyone else has things all figured out, and something is just fundamentally wrong with me.

Do you see the parallel? The double standard that we are helping create with our secrecy and shame?

Nobody has ever told me that if I had more faith or just worked harder at seeing I wouldn't need my contacts anymore.

Nobody has ever begrudged the time I spend at the eye doctor, or the money I spend refilling my contact lenses.

One time I accidentally fell asleep with my contacts in and when I woke up, I thought I had been healed! For real! Sadly, it seems my imperfect eyes are going to be a permanent part of my mortal life, and I will always need medical intervention to deal with them. And here's the really important part—it has never once occurred to me to be ashamed of that.

I also take an anti-anxiety medication. I use it to "correct' my psyche, to help my brain function at its best, just as my contacts do for my eyes. And there is no more reason to be ashamed of taking medication to help my brain work well than there would be to be ashamed of wearing contacts to help my eyes work well.[47]

Elder Jeffrey R. Holland, in his watershed talk on mental illness, said that mental afflictions "are some of the realities of mortal life, and there should be no more shame in acknowledging them than in acknowledging a battle with high blood pressure."[48]

I do put a lot of effort into tapping into spiritual power to help me with my anxiety. I also believe that other approaches are useful as well, particularly when those approaches are combined with a focused reaching for spiritual strength.

This book has obviously focused on the help and healing that can be found through Christ and His Atonement. But often a multi-faceted approach works best. Remember Elder Holland's advice: "If you had appendicitis, God would expect you to seek a priesthood blessing *and* get the best medical care available. So, too, with emotional disorders. Our Father in Heaven expects us to use all of the marvelous gifts He has provided in this glorious dispensation"[49]

An integrated treatment approach to anxiety could include spiritual effort plus any number of other things, such as working with a therapist; having a mindfulness practice; biofeedback; regular exercise; careful, healthful eating habits; relaxation techniques; self-talk; a healthy amount of nightly sleep; and medication, among others. Additional mental health treatments are becoming available all the time as our scientific community learns more about how the mind and body interact. Although these approaches were not included in the scope of this book, they are well worth your time to research and thereby discover which of them belong in your toolbox.

Another helpful tool is to reframe the way you think about yourself. Those with anxiety are often very good at coming up with scenarios of what might happen, how things might go. The "what if" stories we tell ourselves so often. But you know, there's another word for being able to look beyond the present moment and your immediate surroundings. It's called having imagination.

What would happen if, instead of labeling yourself as anxious, you began thinking of yourself as powerfully imaginative? It's true, so if you put it out there enough, your brain would have to believe you. The cool thing is, this power of your imagination can absolutely set you free, because you can imagine the future to be however you want it to be.

You can imagine that a statement you made years ago that you regret has long been forgotten by the person you offended (probably true). You can even imagine that Thanksgiving is going to be completely pleasant and conflict free this year! And if it's not? Then I hereby give you permission to go ahead and worry about that - *while you're at the Thanksgiving table.* But why make yourself miserable twice? If you're going to imagine the future, why not make it a good one? Choose to write yourself happy.

Most of all, please know that having anxiety does not mean something is wrong with you. In fact, never feeling anxious would be the abnormality. Anxiety is a normal part of life for everyone. And, as I've mentioned, feeling anxious is not always a bad thing, although it is always an uncomfortable thing. This is why we seek to eliminate it. If you have a splinter in your finger, you seek to remove it in order to rid yourself of the discomfort as soon as possible. But eliminating all anxiety from our lives should not really be our goal, as that is not a practical endeavor. Some anxiety is useful and does not compete with our faith, but rather aids it. Therefore, we must learn to be masters of our anxiety rather than slaves to it.

Jacob, the great Nephite prophet, received many revelations and much knowledge concerning his people and the future because he had "faith and great anxiety" over them (Jacob 1:5). It's right there in the scriptures, my friends. Faith and anxiety in the same breath, with the powerful, beautiful, spirit-filled outcome of revelation. Reading that scripture is what helped me to understand that not all anxiety is bad or displaces our faith. Other, corroborating scriptures I've found since then are:

2 Nephi 6:3. Jacob again. Another fellow anxiety sufferer, perhaps? I don't know, but if so, he learned to channel it in powerful ways, and that opens up possibilities to my mind that I like to ponder. In this verse, he tells of the great anxiety he has over the welfare of the souls of his people. After which he delivers the first part of a remarkable two-day sermon.

Maybe Jacob came by his anxiety naturally, as his father Lehi also used the word, in 2 Nephi 1:16-17: "And I desire that ye should remember to observe the statutes and the judgments of the Lord; behold, this hath been the anxiety of my soul from the beginning.

My heart hath been weighed down with sorrow from time to time, for I have feared, lest for the hardness of your hearts the Lord your God should come out in the fulness of his wrath upon you, that ye be cut off and destroyed forever."

Notice the language used—anxiety, weighed down, sorrow, fear—all synonyms for or differing degrees of the same emotion. This would be a good example of godly anxiety. Godly anxiety must move us to some sort of sanctifying action. Here, Lehi and Jacob are anxious for the welfare of the souls of those they love, which moves them to preach and exhort them to righteousness.

In contrast, mortal (rather than godly) anxiety often focuses on any aspect of life that feels out of our control. For example, will our child be safe driving around at night? This kind of anxiety might well move us to action of some kind, but it almost certainly will not be sanctifying action. We might over-text our kid to make sure all is well, or stay up worrying, or lash out at a younger child because we are stressed out.

The kind of anxiety we can channel in more productive, sanctifying ways is summed up in D&C 58:27: "Verily I say, men should be anxiously engaged in a good cause, and do many things of their own free will, and bring to pass much righteousness."

Let me give you a practical example. A few years ago, I was asked to teach a class to the young women at Stake Girls' Camp. Although I love to teach and speak, I was anxious about this assignment on many levels. Mainly, I was anxious that I teach those precious girls what the Lord wanted me to teach, and that I would deliver the message in a way that would hold their attention and give the Spirit an opportunity to work on them.

This anxiety led me to take actions such as praying, pondering, writing, revising and practicing. All of which were good, and useful to the ultimate success of the class. Had I not felt some anxiety over the assignment, my natural inclination to laziness would have taken over. I know because I have done that before, when I think I have a speaking assignment in the bag, a no-brainer. Without anxiety, I would have thrown something together at the last minute and it would have been sub-par. The work I put into my Girls' Camp presentation was, in fact, sanctifying for me. In other words, I came out of it just a little holier than I had been before, because I learned some things and had some experiences with the Spirit. This sanctifying result was spurred, at least in part, by a healthy anxiety. A godly anxiety that pushed me to take sanctifying action.

Thus, some anxiety is good for us. It is when we become over-anxious that our anxiety begins to interfere with the gentle ministrations of the Spirit. Let's go back again to the prophet Jacob, who taught us something about this when he said, "Behold, my beloved brethren, I will unfold this mystery unto you; if I do not, by any means, get shaken from my firmness in the Spirit, and stumble because of my over anxiety for you" (Jacob 4:18).

If this sort of over anxiety becomes the norm, then it is time to seek help, including the "faithful pursuit of the time tested devotional practices" recommended by Elder Holland. I have a personal testimony that spiritual effort makes a difference. As President Nelson says, "The Lord loves effort, because *effort brings rewards that can't come without it*,"[50] and with your effort the Spirit will inspire you onto paths of healing and help that are just right for you.

Speaking of paths, there's a road I drive up to the mountains of Arizona when my family and I are ready for a break from the heat of the valley. The drive is beautiful, becoming ever more lush and green as the elevation increases. For a period of time, though, this beautiful scenery was scarred by the after-effects of a large forest fire that ripped through the area, and driving up that stretch of highway became a black and barren experience. The trees were dead. The ground was covered in ashes. It was sad.

Then suddenly one day it was green again. It seemed to happen overnight—plants and trees growing again in an absolutely breathtaking display of life.

Forest fires that are not man-made are called natural disasters, and sometimes we feel like that, too, like we are big ol' natural disasters. But that "disaster" in the forest that looked like the end of the world actually renewed the soil, making it richer and more productive, and the forest ended up even more beautiful than it had been before. This is what awaits us. If you feel like your life is something of a disaster, take heart—you are completely normal! And not only that, you are participating in the plan of salvation in exactly the way you were meant to do. The failures we have, the embarrassments, the mistakes, and even the disasters combine with the grace of our Lord Jesus

Christ to enrich our lives and renew our spirits and eventually make us into divinely beautiful kings and queens, priests and priestesses.

That is who you are.

You are not your anxiety. You are a divine child of Heavenly Parents who sometimes feels anxious.

You are not faithless. Nor are you fearless. But you don't have to be fearless to be faithful.

You are not a quitter. You face anxiety every day, and you are still here, trying.

You are not unlovable. You are loved endlessly, unconditionally, unchangeably.

You are not hopelessly broken. You are human. And you will be perfect in Christ one day.

You are not the sum of your mistakes, but the sum of your mistakes *and* your triumphs *and* your divine nature. All of which adds up to one mighty choice individual: you.

You are not hopeless. You are waiting in hope for the day when "the spirits of those who are righteous are received into a state of happiness, which is called paradise, a state of rest, a state of peace, where they shall rest from all their troubles and from all care, and sorrow" (Alma 40:12).

I testify that as we come unto Christ, exercising our spiritual will, exerting our best efforts, and seeking help from all the resources we have been blessed with, we can find that peace and rest not just in the eternities, but today, this very day.

Endnotes

1 Maxwell, Neal A. "The Seventh Commandment: A Shield," *Ensign*, November 2001, para. 13.

2 Burrup, Lyle J. "Anxiety and Anxiety Disorders," *Ensign*, March 2017, para. 3-4.

3 McClendon, Debra Theobold https://www.thechurchnews.com/living-faith/2018-08-23/healthy-vs-debilitating-anxiety-and-the-best-ways-to-cope-9145, para. 9.

4 Holland, Jeffrey R., "Like a Broken Vessel," *Ensign*, November 2013, para. 6.

5 *Just Like You*, https://www.churchofjesuschrist.org/media/video/2019-05-1000-just-like-you?lang=eng).

6 Gong, Gerrit W., "Good Shepherd, Lamb of God," *Ensign*, May 2019, para. 2.

7 Soares, Ulisses S., "Always Remember Him," BYU Devotional, Feb. 5, 2019.

8 Boyack, Merrilee, "Helping Others Receive the Lord's Healing," *Ensign*, June 2019, para. 19.

9 Eubank, Sharon, "Christ: The Light That Shines in Darkness," *Ensign*, May 2019, para. 14

10 Ibid.

11 Nelson, Wendy Watson "…My Soul Delighteth in the Covenants of the Lord," BYU Women's Conference, 2015.

12   Clark, Kim B. "Look Unto Jesus Christ," *Ensign*, May 2019, para. 21.

13   Gong, Gerrit W., "Always Remember Him," *Ensign*, May 2016, para. 18.

14   Bednar, David A., "Bear Up Their Burden With Ease," *Ensign*, May 2014, para. 20, 26.

15   Hilton, Joni, "The Problem With Pondering," *Meridian Magazine, Line Upon Line*, October 3, 2013.

16   Staheli, Donald L., "Obedience, Life's Great Challenge," *Ensign*, May 1998, para. 12.

17   Hales, Robert D., "If Ye Love Me, Keep My Commandments," *Ensign*, May 2014, para. 28.

18   Monson, Thomas S., "Obedience Brings Blessings," *Ensign*, May 2013, para. 32.

19   Griffith, Jessica, "You, the Youth and the Mutual Theme", *Ensign*, January 2018, para. 19.

20   Cordon, Bonnie H., "Trust in the Lord, and Lean Not," *Ensign*, May 2017, para. 6.

21   Scott, Richard G., "Trust In The Lord," *Ensign*, November 1995, para. 7.

22   Kapp, Ardeth G., "The Holy Scriptures: Letters From Home," *Ensign*, November 1985, para. 11.

23   Young, Ellie, "The Transformative Power of Covenants," BYU Devotional, June 11, 2019.

24   Holland, Patricia. "Fear Not." BYU Devotional, Sept. 15, 1987.

25   Stallings, Mary, "Olive Tree Allegory," Come Follow Me Daily, March 17, 2020 https://www.facebook.com/comefollowmedaily/photos/a.355166861649397/540064579826290/.

26   Nielson, Brent H., "Can We Live "After the Manner of Happiness"?" *Ensign*, September 2016, para. 28.

27   Monson, Thomas S., "Be Of Good Cheer," *Ensign*, May 2009, para. 4.

28 Holland, Jeffrey R., "Like a Broken Vessel," *Ensign,* November 2013, para. 14.

29 https://history.churchofjesuschrist.org/event/marjorie-pay-hinckley?lang=eng.

30 Andersen, Neil L., "You Know Enough," *Ensign,* November 2008, para. 14.

31 See Stevenson, Gary E., "5 Ways to Conquer Fear," *New Era,* February 2017.

32 Benson, Ezra Taft, "Cleansing the Inner Vessel," *Ensign,* May 1986, para. 33.

33 Hinckley, Gordon B., "The Environment of Our Homes," *Ensign,* June 1985, para. 11.

34 Clark, Gregory, "Some Lessons on Faith and Fear," BYU Devotional, May 10, 2008.

35 Uchtdorf, Dieter F., "Perfect Love Casteth Out Fear," *Ensign,* May 2017, para. 52.

36 Marriott, Neill F., "Abiding in God and Repairing the Breach," *Ensign,* November 2017, para. 16.

37 *Lord, I Would Follow Thee,* Hymns: 220

38 Marriott, Neill F., "Abiding in God and Repairing the Breach," *Ensign,* November 2017, para. 9.

39 Ibid., para. 12.

40 Available as on audio talk on CD from Deseret Book.

41 Rasband, James, "Ensuring A Righteous Judgment," *Ensign,* May 2020, para. 17.

42 Scott, Richard G., "The Path to Peace and Joy," *Ensign,* November 2000, para. 24.

43 Nielson, Brent H., "Can We Live After the Manner of Happiness?", *Ensign,* September 2016, para. 10.

44 Eubank, Sharon, "Turn On Your Light," *Ensign,* November 2017, para. 14

45   Renlund, Dale G., "Latter-Day Saints Keep on Trying," *Ensign*, May 2015, para. 1.

46   Reeves, Linda S., "The Great Plan of Redemption," *Ensign*, November 2016, para. 1.

47   Thank you to life coach Jody Moore for this insight.

48   Holland, Jeffrey R., "Like a Broken Vessel," *Ensign*, November 2013, para. 1.

49   Ibid., para. 8

50   Joy D. Jones, "An Especially Noble Calling," *Ensign*, May 2020, para. 8.

Made in the USA
Las Vegas, NV
30 June 2022

50943007R00057